Dismantled

How Love and Psychedelics Broke a Clergyman Apart and Put Him Back Together

BRUCE SANGUIN

Foreword by Andrew Feldmár

Published by Viriditas Press

Book and cover design by Rayola Creative
Cover image by Bill Oxford

This book is available in most bookstores, and world-wide through online booksellers.
ISBN: 978-0-9948870-2-3 (print)
ISBN: 978-0-9948870-3-0 (digital)

For all inquiries about this book, please contact the author at www.brucesanguin.ca

Bruce Sanguin's *Dismantled* is a book of changes, eloquent inquiry, and a study of faith, belief, and epistemology — how do we know what we think we know? Alphonso Lingis says in *The Community of Those Who Have Nothing in Common*, that "One enters into conversation in order to become an other for the other." *Dismantled* is a conversation, and now the reader gets to be in on it. May the truth show itself between us all in its infinite, novel and surprising faces.

— **Andrew Feldmár, Psychotherapist**

Dismantled is a remarkable book of highly applicable wisdom. Bruce Sanguin has done much of the inner transformative work anyone interested in spiritual healing needs to do. Based on this inner work and his many years working with others, he brings to bear a powerful gift for elucidating essential insights and truths about the work of awakening, delivering it all in language both eloquent and accessible. Too often to count I marveled at sentences that jumped off the page with crystalline clarity. And just as often, I found myself nodding in agreement at experiences and insights that rang true and resonated personally. Brilliant.

— **Stephen Gray, author of *Returning to Sacred World:***
A Spiritual Toolkit for the Emerging Reality

Once a decade a book grabs me by the throat and drags me to the end before I've had a chance to protest. Beautiful. Honest. Insightful. Haunting. Necessary. This is Bruce Sanguin the psychotherapist at the top of his practice and the human being at his most authentic. I hope this book finds its way into the hands of the courageous souls who are ready to say yes to their greatest adventure and the battle to actualize their truest selves.

— **Ryan Meeks, Founder of Eastlake Church, Seattle WA**

Bruce Sanguin's story is raw, open, compelling and courageous. He lets us in on some of the most terrifying and intimate moments of his own "dismantling" with the help of psychedelics, a trusted shaman and a psycho-therapist. He models the centrality of deep, conscious integration of these experiences.

Sanguin weaves together aspects of psychological theory, including trauma, attachment and family systems, while drawing upon his background as a Christian minister to offer fresh interpretations of who Jesus was and the depth of his teachings. The books ends by providing a helpful healing map to uncover and transform unconscious negative beliefs that were formed in response to early trauma.

— **Toni Pieroni, Clinical Counsellor, MA, RCC**

CONTENTS

God speaks to each of us as he makes us,
then walks with us silently out of the night.
These are the words we dimly hear:
You, sent out beyond your recall,
go to the limits of your longing.
Embody me.
Flare up like a flame and make big shadows
I can move in.
Let everything happen to you: beauty and terror.
Just keep going. No feeling is final.
Don't let yourself lose me.
Nearby is the country they call life.
You will know it by its seriousness.
Give me your hand.

— **Rilke, *Book of Hours*, I, 59**

Foreword

Psychedelics, entheogens, empathogens, hallucinogens, indigenous medicines, synthetic drugs, shamans, therapists, transcendence, regression, psyche, spirit and body, vomit, tears and laughter, sessions and ceremonies — who will be a guide to the perplexed? I've been meandering in these woods ever since 1967, for over fifty years. Talking with R. D. Laing about experiences in a variety of *altered states of consciousness*, very quickly we arrived at a curious impasse. "I grant you that you have had the experiences you've recounted," he said, "I have no doubt, whatsoever. I am certain of the experiences I have had and some of them are similar to yours. However, *what do they mean?*" And so, we have to live with radical uncertainty. Do LSD, 5-MEO-DMT teach us about death? About crucifixion and resurrection? Is there a beneficent grandmother conjured up by ayahuasca who is courted by the shaman's eerie *icaros*? Are there curious intelligences to commune with under the influence of DMT? Am I a Chinese emperor dreaming that I am a butterfly, or am I a butterfly who dreams that he is a Chinese emperor? Does it matter?

The major benefit of Buddhist meditation, *vipassana* for instance, is to transmute automatic habit patterns into heartfelt responses. Although we are existentially condemned to freedom, in order to thrive in less than optimal circumstances in infancy, childhood and adolescence, we are left with habits that helped us to survive but are useless or harmful in the here and now, where war is actually over. Under the influence of powerful substances and in the company of experienced Sherpas, the self-serving viruses of our bio-computer get loosened and cleaned out. Perhaps the imagery doesn't matter in the least. The benefit is the freedom gained in the wake of dissipated habits. Authenticity arises from the heart, from heartfelt, spontaneous and candid responsiveness.

Bruce Sanguin's *Dismantled* is a book of changes, eloquent inquiry, and a study of faith, belief, and epistemology — how do we know what we think we know? Alphonso Lingis says in *The Community of Those Who Have Nothing in Common*, that "One enters into conversation in order to become an other for the other." *Dismantled* is a conversation, and now the reader gets to be in on it. May the truth show itself between us all in its infinite, novel and surprising faces.

— **Andrew Feldmár**

Introduction

DISMANTLE: *"To take a machine apart or to come apart into separate pieces; to get rid of a system or organization, usually over a period of time."*

MANTLE: *"The responsibilities of an important position or job; a layer of something that covers a surface."*

— **Cambridge Dictionary**

Love and psychedelics are effective dismantlers. The mantle of the personality that I wore to protect my heart was no match for love when it showed up. Psychedelics finished the job, revealing everything in me that was not up for the rigors of deep intimacy. "I" came apart. Or was it "me," not my essential nature but the meticulously constructed personality formed to help me survive early heartbreak?

Externally, the mantle I wore as an ordained clergyman was also removed. When it became clear that the mandate of love was at odds with the piety of a handful of souls in the congregation I served, I knew that it was time to hang up the vestments for good. I gifted my stoles and liturgical gowns to a newly ordained friend. It all seemed relatively painless at the time. But I was fooling myself — a well-developed competency of my ego.

Two years after I left congregational ministry I was attending an ayahuasca ceremony (which I describe below). When a woman discovered my former identity, she asked if I would baptize her. She wanted to redeem a negative childhood experience of church. Her visions were telling her that she needed to be baptized even though she wasn't a Christian.

A dismantled clergyman and a non-Christian climbed their way up the side of a mountain in the jungles of Mexico to a pool of water by a waterfall. Five other women, constituting an ad hoc congregation, chanted and burned incense. This woman climbed into the pool. I laid one hand on her back and the other under her head as she immersed herself in the mountain pool. She resurfaced, a new creation. Never in all my years as an "official" clergyman had I participated in such moving and authentic ceremony. Afterwards, walking up the steps to my cabin, I broke down in tears, feeling the grief of all the layers coming off. This was anything but painless. I had lost everything in this stripping down but gained my soul.

When I first read the definition of "dismantle" I almost rejected it as a book title because it usually refers to a machine. But it's perfect. When we are conditioned by past events, particularly trauma, our freedom as humans is limited. Robot-like, we move through our lives appearing to make choices. But the big choices, like

> *Do I commit to being here in this life?*
> *Am I all-in when it comes to love?*
> *I up for the inherent intensity of life, moment by moment?*

These are soul-sized choices, and the truth was that my soul hadn't really come on line, until love and psychedelics began the gracious, excruciating work of breaking me apart. The machine was being disassembled. The liberated human, hidden under the mantle of the role and the rules of survival, was ready to try again.

In *Choruses from the Rock,* T. S. Eliot asks, "Where is the Life we have lost in living?" The poem is a lament for a time before modernity reduced humanity to "decent godless people: their only monument the asphalt road and a thousand lost golf balls." The asphalt road leads always away from community, and the thousand lost golf balls describe a species that has mastered the art of distraction. Eliot chalks our contemporary alienation up to the loss of God. Perhaps, but I think it starts closer to home, with childhood trauma.

When we receive the message that we are not lovable in our natural, spontaneous and innocent condition, we go into physical, emotional and psychic shock. This message may be overt (that is, it may take the form of actual physical or sexual abuse) or covert (in which case it takes the form of neglect; a parent withholding love or maintaining an emotional distance; or a parent using us to support his or her narcissistic needs). Because we cannot live without knowing we are loved, we adopt a survival strategy, becoming whoever we believe our abusive parent(s) needs us to be. The strategy works to help us navigate childhood, but when we become adults, the persona (our mantle) we developed to appease our parent(s) drastically diminishes the quality of our life and intimacy.

The heartbreak we too often feel as children establishes the foundation for a life of alienation. We become survivalists; our only goal is learning how to make the hurt stop. This involves cutting off feelings and sensations that were overwhelming to us as infants, toddlers and children. The cost of this loss of feeling, including the loss of love for oneself, is lost life. When the "real" hurts too much, we learn to live at a distance from our body, from Earth and from each other.

When love fails us, we abandon what is real and true, in the world and in ourselves, and soon we forget the reality and the truth. We never learn what it means to be creative, free and loving. The self we forge in this state of amnesia is a stand-in, a caricature of our real self, settling for the mock-up world that is on offer. No longer guided by inner feelings and sensations, the self loses track of its own needs and wants, taking its cues from others, learning how to please, ever alert to what is expected at any given moment. This alienated self is bombarded by advertisements only too willing to tell it what to do. We are no longer initiated into our deep purpose by the tribe. Community thus becomes not a resource to support our unique vision but rather the place where our unconscious, unmet needs wreak havoc.

Indeed, the algorithms of Facebook, that great online community, push us into our superficial purpose — to consume. We thus become shoppers and robots, not humans. Getting one's life back requires resistance, and resistance starts with becoming conscious of what broke our hearts. Only then can we be free to be human.

This alienated self, the stand-in, was always meant to be a temporary life raft, something that would help us survive childhood. But we get attached to it. It becomes us. We become it. If we're lucky, the raft will get swamped. When it starts to break apart, we are left to sink or swim. The distant shore beckons. There is no guarantee that we will reach it, but the desperate desire to live and feel the ground beneath our feet again is a sign that the self that has been lost wants another chance.

Ayahuasca first shattered my raft and then threw me a lifeline. This ancient tea, concocted by shamans in the jungles of the Amazon, tore back the curtain on my psyche and peeled away my defenses, revealing what years of introspection and therapy had not. The sacred medicine took the guesswork out of it. I *knew*, deep in my bones, that what was being revealed was true! Thus began my journey with this healing medicine, a journey that continues to this day.

Besides drinking ayahuasca, I began a series of intensive four-hour psychedelic psychotherapy sessions, using MDMA (commonly known as ecstasy) and LSD, over the course of two years. My wise and compassionate therapist, Andrew Feldmar, accompanied me as guide. These sessions tended to focus more directly on intimacy and trust. Unlike the ayahuasca ceremonies I attended, which occurred in a group of up to twenty-five people and placed a high premium on self-reliance, these one-on-one psychotherapy sessions were all about learning to connect with "the other" as a source of support. The dynamics of love and hate, approach and avoidance, tenderness and rage, connection and alienation, attachment and isolation were in play. With my therapist I recapitulated my earliest experiences of love and its failures. The wounds that I had denied and ignored for too many decades began to heal.

One of the reasons I am sharing my story is to add my voice to the burgeoning movement of people who have experienced the healing power of entheogens ("generating God within") like ayahuasca, MDMA and LSD. There is an irrational fear of psychedelics and various vision-generating plant medicines, which has been intentionally cultivated. When taken in the context of sacred ceremonies or with a competent therapist, these substances are powerful medicines. (I've never taken them recreationally, so I cannot speak to their healing potential outside these contexts.) They have the potential to heal and spiritually evolve our species.

Another reason to write this book is that I want to be a spokesperson for the silent majority out there who suffer in silence but who aren't members of the target groups — the most traumatized and vulnerable among us — who are the focus of most research and treatment. I believe it is right that the bulk of resources are directed to these individuals, but it doesn't mean the pain of the rest of us should be ignored.

I wouldn't have been eligible for any of these research projects because my life appeared "normal." But I've observed that what gets labeled "normal," "well-adjusted," "successful" — choose your adjective — is actually an alarmingly degraded expression of what it means to be human.

Early childhood failures of love establish the defense structures that enable us to thrive in a social, economic and political system that itself reflects a deep alienation from the authentically human. When we begin the healing process, we simultaneously awaken to the dehumanizing nature of our systems, from our hostile birth practices to our death phobia. This alienation is reflected in universities whose curricula are increasingly influenced by corporations; in social policy that does not support young parents; in an economic system that has entrenched inequality; in a corporate food system that ends in a grocery store selling food that isn't actually food, and that is certainly not clean, sustainable or healthy; and in a health care system that refuses to subsidize so-called alternative practices that focus on prevention. As we awaken to a deep love for self, it becomes increasingly offensive to participate in these alienated and alienating social systems and structures.

This personal and systemic alienation from the deeply human is reflected in the soaring rates of addiction. As Canadian music icon Bruce Cockburn puts it: "The trouble with normal is it always gets worse." It is my conviction that personal healing will lead to the healing of these social systems. In this sense, personal work is a foundation for the work to achieve social justice and equity.

Rev. Bruce

Only a year before I began my journey with these medicines, psychedelics were far from my mind. For twenty-eight years I had worked in the church as a pastor. Sure, I was intrigued by the early accounts of Aldous Huxley and others describing their experience of mescaline and LSD. But I never seriously imagined tripping myself.

For the last seventeen of my years as a pastor, I worked with a congregation in Vancouver, Canada. Canadian Memorial United Church is a liberal congregation. We were LGBT positive, took the Bible seriously but never literally and, in sync with the United Church of Canada's ethos, we were committed to social justice. Mostly I liked my work but there were a few downsides.

The most frustrating part of the work was dealing with individuals who were unconsciously taking out their own childhood wounds on others in the community, and on me. As the designated leader, a pastor is on the receiving end of unconscious projections — individuals expect you to make up for the love they didn't get growing up. One elderly woman stalked me every Sunday morning for fifteen years, just to tell me how disappointed she was in me. A team of volunteers made it their Sunday-morning job to keep her away from me. Other people would walk away from the community mysteriously, never to return. Only later did I discover that they had taken personally what I thought was an innocuous comment. Because these individuals learned as children that they could not confront their parents, they chose as adults to re-enact this learned passivity.

The Canadian Memorial congregation was unusual. It wasn't dying. As the largest Protestant denomination in Canada, the United Church of Canada has been in decline since reaching its zenith during the 1960s. But this church was slowly growing. More importantly, we were mostly happy and alive. In the last few years of my time there I was accepting an increasing number of invitations to travel and give talks and workshops focused on my books about evolutionary theology and spirituality.[1] I suggested that I move to half-time work and hire another person to cover the pastoral and administrative gap my absence would create.

What the congregation didn't know was that my marriage was in its death throes. I concealed this publicly, but for years I was tormented. I knew that whatever love I had once felt for my wife was gone. I was sure

---

1   Before coming to Canadian Memorial, I had experienced my own awakening, coming to an awareness that the evolutionary process was not the meaningless, random affair it was made out to be by neo-Darwinian materialism. Rather, I contended, a mysterious creativity and intelligence was non-coercively moving in and through evolution, biased toward an increase in love and reflecting the "heart of the cosmos" itself. I persuaded this congregation to re-imagine "church" in alignment with this possibility. In this form, the real action of church would be to shape the future as personalized occasions of this evolutionary consciousness rather than looking back over our shoulders at what happened a couple of thousand years ago, as if Jesus of Nazareth did all the heavy lifting.

there must be something wrong with me since I was unable to love. I was enduring the relationship for all the wrong reasons: financial security, shame at the possibility of another failed marriage, and an arrogant will that believed I could make anything work.

While I was on sabbatical in 2013 I made a difficult decision to end the relationship. A handful of congregational members chose to believe my former wife's version of events and circulated a petition that would have triggered a review of my leadership. My leadership had never been questioned before this, and the board of Canadian Memorial knew the accusations were baseless. But I refused to get involved in a "he-said, she-said" scenario or spend the next few years dealing with this kind of pettiness. Instead I resigned and took early retirement.

Some might call this taking the high road. I prefer this spin on the story myself. But an early ayahuasca ceremony revealed a more complex and less flattering truth. What I didn't know then, but do now, was that I carried an unconscious fear of rejection. Frustration from early childhood rejections was pent up and waiting to be released. In the face of this petition, I impetuously flipped the finger at "mother" church before she could reject me. Because I was unconscious of the impact of childhood trauma, my rage was misdirected. I would discover in psychedelic psychotherapy sessions that it was actually meant for my real mother.

I suspect that a pattern of cutting off at the first sign of rejection — a trauma reaction — prevented me from making a smoother, more elegant transition. My years with this congregation were fruitful, and we shared deep affection and respect. If I had it to do over again, knowing what I now know after my journey with psychedelics, I would have taken my leave with a little more equanimity. Still, it *was* time to leave.

In John's gospel, when Jesus is getting ready to check out, he tells his disciples that there are many "rooms" in his Father's house. One of them (and only one) is the institutional church. By the end it was a room too small for where my soul wanted to take me. I'm grateful for the time I had in the church and for those who enriched my life. My psychotherapy office is now my new sanctuary, a ceremonial space for grief and the reclamation of the true self by courageous souls.

In the Beginning…

I was born in a hospital in Kindersley, a small town in central Saskatche-wan. The temperatures are extreme in both winter (the record low is −45 degrees C) and summer (the record high, 41.7 degrees C). A twenty-foot Silverliner trailer sheltered our family of five from these conditions. An older sister and a younger brother sandwiched me by fifteen months on each side.

I cannot imagine the challenges that my parents faced. My mother was nineteen when she had my sister, and my father was twenty-four. He was a teacher, but working the oil rigs paid more in the 1950s. We hauled the trailer behind a brand-new '55 Ford Fairlane, chasing the oil. To this day I gag at the smell of diesel fuel. My father's favourite pastime when he'd fin-ished his shift on the rig was playing poker and drinking with the boys. My mother spent many nights leaving us kids with God knows who and hauling his butt out of the bar.

Like the weather, my overwhelmed mother ran hot and cold. To me, her heart seemed wintry cold. I experienced an absence of tenderness, gentleness and genuine affection. I accepted this as normal. Her temper could also flare like the July prairie sun, particularly toward us boys. During an ayahuasca ceremony many years later, I discovered that I believed my life was in danger if I couldn't figure out what she wanted.

At my mother's insistence and to her credit, my father (to his credit) cashed in his poker chips, took up contract bridge and gave up drinking. We moved to Winnipeg, Manitoba, to live with my grandmother. I was five years old. A younger sister was born shortly thereafter, so my mother had four children under the age of six. Eight years later our youngest sister was born. When I was in grade seven, we welcomed a basketball teammate into our home. He became like another brother to us all.

When the true story of these early years started to emerge I felt com-passion, for myself and for my parents. They were young and poor and coping with their own inherited family trauma. They did the best they could. Yet "the best they could" broke my heart. I lived with a broken heart all my life but, strangely, didn't know it. Outwardly I was the golden boy: well-adjusted, lots of friends, exceptional athlete, good student and suc-cessful in my career. A few people, intuitive types, felt my sadness, but I denied it.

The Truth Shall Knock You Upside the Head

I don't tell my story to point fingers at my parents or at the people who didn't recognize my troubles. I tell it to show how our culture still doesn't take the lasting impact of early childhood trauma, failed attachment, emotional neglect and physical abuse seriously. This is because culture takes its cues from science, and science, in the form of the psychiatric profession, has been slow to believe that childhood emotional trauma has any impact on mental and emotional health.

The American Psychiatric Association rejected the idea of a diagnosis of developmental trauma disorder in May 2011, stating: "The notion that early childhood adverse experiences lead to substantial developmental disruptions is more clinical intuition than a research-based fact. There is no known evidence of developmental disruptions that were preceded in time in a causal fashion by any type of trauma syndrome."

This fails to take into account exhaustive research by many researchers, including psychiatrist Bessel van der Kolk, along with a 1997 study by the Centers for Disease Control and Kaiser Permanente, in which 17,421 patients volunteered to respond to a questionnaire on "adverse childhood experiences" or ACEs (a catchall phrase referring to physical, emotional and sexual abuse; physical and emotional neglect; and household dysfunctions such as mental illness, domestic violence, divorce, substance abuse and incarcerated relatives).[2] These were largely white, middle-class, professional people who could afford health insurance in the United States and would be considered well-adjusted citizens. The results show that childhood trauma is far more prevalent than we imagined. Here are some of the most significant findings:

- Almost two-thirds of those interviewed reported at least one ACE in their past.

People with six or more ACEs:

- Were likely to die twenty years earlier, on average

---

2   "Adverse Childhood Experiences (ACEs)," on the Centers for Disease Control and Prevention website (https://www.cdc.gov/violenceprevention/acestudy/), 2016.

- Had a 4,600 percent increase in the likelihood of that they would become injection drug users

People with four or more ACEs:

- Had a 460 percent increase in the likelihood of depression
- Had a 1,220 percent increase in the likelihood they would attempt suicide
- Had a 500 percent increase in rates of self-reported alcoholism

The research shows a clear, causal relationship between ACEs and disrupted neurodevelopment; social, emotional and cognitive impairment; the adoption of self-harming behavior (including suicide); disease; disability; social problems; and early death.[3]

Most of us, myself included, lead double lives until we take our childhood failures of love seriously. The extreme version of a double life is dissociative identity disorder (formerly multiple personality disorder), which is an expression of absolute dissociation from early suffering. My splitting off wasn't nearly so severe. But I did master the ability to cut off the feelings and sensations in my body. I did learn to close my heart to deep intimacy. I fled earth and body, and took flight into thought and spirit.

When I began to use psychedelics, this medicine revealed to me that the heart is a fragile and sensitive instrument. We are so open to give and receive love that when we discover our parents aren't really up to the task, we are devastated. We don't have a name for it as babies and toddlers, but love is the whole enchilada. In the absence of a steady, caring and joyful presence signaling to us that we're a delight to be with, life is intolerably painful. We shut down, and if my life is anywhere close to the norm, we may never open up again to the deep joy and intensity of life. This toned-down version of life, expressed through a contracted self, we learn to accept as "normal." At least, our false selves see it as normal. It wasn't until I felt tenderness from within for my self on the medicine that I realized what I had been missing.

---

3 A helpful illustration of the ACE pyramid, which shows how "ACES are strongly related to development of risk factors for disease, and well-being throughout the life course," can be found at the same CDC website (https://www.cdc.gov/violenceprevention/acestudy/about.html).

The ways these failures of love show up in our adult life vary considerably. Before my experience with psychedelics I would have sworn on a stack of Bibles that these early failures played no part in my behavior as an adult. How wrong I was!

In one extended psychedelic session with my therapist, I took MDMA. I was feeling wonderfully relaxed, connected and loving toward him. Then he reminded me that if I also intended to take the LSD, it was time.

In a millisecond I was flooded with panic. I felt sick to my stomach. My whole body was seized by anxiety.

I told him what was happening and he guided me to look within. I saw that when he reminded me it was time to take the LSD, I was certain he was doing so just to break the connection with me. In my fantasy, I believed he wanted to get rid of me as I sank deeper into an altered state. He did not want to be with me, and drugging me was his way out.

This was clearly a memory of an earlier time in my life, when my mother found ways to disappear me or disappear herself before I was ready. I haven't checked this out with my mother, but I do know it was common in those days to give babies and toddlers sedatives to calm them down — and give mothers a break. So my experience with my therapist replayed an early experience of being cut off from connection before I was ready. As I dived deeper, I realized that I had a pattern of prematurely cutting off intimate connection in anticipation of reliving this trauma.

This was subtle. Anybody observing me at the time might have thought my actions and responses were innocuous and benign — unless they were a psychologist who had researched infant and toddler attachment styles. The failures of attachment I had experienced with my mother, though subtle, had affected me for a lifetime.

Over one hundred years ago, Freud discovered that much of our behavior is shaped below the level of conscious awareness. We carry on as if we are free actors in the drama of life, believing that we have written our own script. But unless we uncover those deeper motivations, we are never truly free. Today's materialist philosophers and scientists are likewise convinced that freedom is an illusion: we are programmed by survival instincts and genetic material that uses us to reproduce itself, lost in a universe that is itself random.

This   unconscious lack of freedom is the subject of a great many films, including *The Bourne Conspiracy*, *The Manchurian Candidate* and *The Matrix*. But in these films the powers pulling the levers in the lives of unsuspecting protagonists are malevolent outsiders — the CIA, power-mongering corporations, political parties and computer-generated programs. There's a truth that lies much closer to home. In the privacy of our families, failures of love and outright acts of violence condemn children to live lives that are not their own. We construct false selves in order to survive. As long as our inner survivalist is running the show, we can never be truly free.

Maybe the greatest cover-up of all time is the conspiracy of silence around the family as an institution. We are still loath to question the sanctity of an institution that has inflicted untold violence upon children.

Truth alone sets us free. The discovery of this truth is the most important journey we'll ever take. But I'm not referring to a philosophical or spiritual truth. It's the truth of our own suffering inflicted by those charged with loving us. Discovering this truth unlocks the prison door of denial and liberates us to finally write our own stories.

Case in point: the story of how I "answered the call" and became a minister. During my undergraduate year I stumbled on Transcendental Meditation. This was strange for a jock. My buddies thought I had lost my mind. For three years I tapped into a deep peace as I sat twice a day in meditation. I told my mother that I intended to take an advanced course. She pleaded with me to postpone the decision and come with her to hear an evangelical preacher. That night at the rally I "gave my life to Jesus." The die was cast for a career in the church. Well-meaning friends then brainwashed me with teachings that had nothing to do with Jesus: "Idle minds are the devil's playground," don't you know? I dropped a practice that I loved and which was life enhancing.

There's nobody to blame here. My mother did what protective mothers do. As an adult I made my own decisions. But I didn't understand that below the surface a frightened toddler was in on that decision. I needed to please my mother. The toddler was also wary about waking the sleeping dragon that I knew in my mother as an infant and toddler. I call my actions contortion through conformance. I contorted myself by conforming to expectations that were set down and enforced before I had a say in the matter.

This is the hallmark of a traumatized soul. For me, the past unconsciously led to a decision that shaped my entire life.

That said, I don't regret my career in the church. Although my ecclesiastical career was made with the help of my inner toddler, there was something right about it. For one thing, I got to grapple with Jesus of Nazareth. At various stages in the evolution of my faith he's been saviour, Jewish rabbi, wisdom teacher, shaman and my own inner Christ nature. While I have quit the church, Jesus has not quit me.

Jesus's teachings took on new meanings in light of my psychedelic experiences. When I share the spiritual dimension of these experiences, I primarily (but not exclusively) refer to Christianity. This is not because I believe Christianity is more true or valid than other religions or spiritual paths. It is simply a matter of familiarity. I do not believe there is a single Absolute Reality or Being hiding behind reality or above it. Rather, as we participate intensively with the world as it is and in our lives as they are, the Great Mystery that is indeterminate, fluid and radically relational is disclosed in multiple and unique ways.

Psychedelic journeys have not been about riding a unicorn off into the cosmos, at least not for me. Sure, I've had visions, amazing transcendent visions. And I've been transported into the mind and heart of Source. I'm grateful for these experiences when they happen. I describe some of them in the book. But they are gravy.

What drove me to psychedelics more than anything else was love. I wanted to get to the bottom of why I could be such an asshole with the woman I loved. I had ended two previous marriages, and then when I found the love of my life, I turned my life inside out to be with her. She was literally an answer to prayer. I wanted, above all, to know uninhibited love.

But once I was with her, trouble started. In the crucible of this love fire, feelings emerged that up to this point in my life I had kept in check. I raged when she challenged me. Sometimes hate was as strong as love. When we fought, I couldn't stay connected. I was hypersensitive. Dark moods overtook me. I left the house in anger, once for two days. It made no rational sense because I had found my soul mate. Yet I couldn't deny that when I looked at her, I saw my parents' ghosts from the past. I was in danger of sabotaging what I most wanted. I knew I had work to do to make myself fit for love.

As I tracked the thread of frustration with love to its source in childhood, the great unraveling began. The garment that I believed to be my "self" came apart as the whole story came out — and it wasn't the story I had been telling myself for so many years. Psychedelics helped me suspend my well-honed defense system and allowed this disrupting narrative to surface.

Getting Past the Stigma

Fortunately, not everybody suffers from painful childhoods. Many parents provide a stable and loving environment during the formative years. If you are one of the lucky ones who received such loving acceptance, this book may not be for you, except perhaps as a curiosity.

A word of caution is in order, though. Before my journey with these medicines I would have identified myself as one of these lucky ones. The mechanisms of denial and repression, as we'll see, are stubborn. They were put in place for a good reason. That said, this isn't everybody's work to do, and psychedelics aren't for everybody. But they are an invaluable aid for those, like me, who need to go deeper into why we limit ourselves so severely when it comes to matters of the heart.

I, too, grew up thinking psychedelics were bad and that only bad people used them. They caused people to swan dive off roofs. In my mind there were only three groups in high school: the jocks, the potheads and the geeks. I was a jock. And while I occasionally smoked pot, I bought none. Only the true potheads bought the stuff. When I smoked I worried that I might become one of them. I didn't know a single soul in Winnipeg who took LSD. I tried a low dose of mushrooms once, which I allude to in this story, but there was never much danger of my turning into a psychonaut. I was brainwashed to believe that psychedelics led to madness or criminality.

Richard Nixon can take credit for the effectiveness of this propaganda. His War on Drugs (1968) spread paranoia about psychedelics, establishing the stigma that lingers today in mainstream North American society. From the start it was a political strategy and not evidence-based. Dan Baum wrote an article for *Harper's Magazine* revealing the strategy.[4] He tracked

---

4   Dan Baum, "Legalize It All: How to Win the War on Drugs," *Harper's Magazine*, April 2016.

down Nixon's domestic policy advisor, John Ehrlichman, who was also a Watergate co-conspirator. Before he could get the question out, Ehrlichman gave Baum the straight goods: "The Nixon campaign in 1968, and the Nixon White House after that, had two enemies: the antiwar left and black people. You understand what I'm saying? We knew we couldn't make it illegal to be either against the war or black, but by getting the public to associate the hippies with marijuana and blacks with heroin, and then criminalizing both heavily, we could disrupt those communities. We could arrest their leaders, raid their homes, break up their meetings, and vilify them night after night on the evening news. Did we know we were lying about the drugs? Of course we did."

Research into LSD was encouraging before this big chill. For millennia humans have been ingesting psychedelic plants ceremonially — mushrooms, peyote, iboga, ayahuasca, morning glory seeds, poppy seeds (opium) and countless other plants. For most of our history these plants were considered gifts of the gods, made available to humans to open them to the divine, within and without.

Mushrooms, for example, show up in iconic Christian images of the first few centuries AD. Ergot, a psychedelic fungal parasite (a precursor to LSD), or magic mushrooms likely powered the Eleusinian Mysteries, rituals held annually in ancient Greece. In ancient Hindu ceremonies, a plant extract, soma, opened the minds and hearts of participants to eternity. Long before this, Mongolian shamans were using *Amanita muscaria* (a species of psychedelic mushrooms), and African shamans used the root of the plant iboga to help participants enter the invisible realms, connect to the ancestors and receive healing.

In his comprehensive study *Poisons Sacrés, Ivresses Divines (Sacred Poisons, Divine Raptures),* historian and theologian Phillippe de Félice wrote about the immemorial connection between religion and psychedelics. He says that the use of these "poisons sacrés" is "extraordinarily widespread…The practices in this volume can be observed in every region of the earth, among indigenous people, no less than among those who have reached the high pitch of 'civilization.' We are therefore dealing not with exceptional facts, which might justifiably be overlooked, but with a general and, in the widest sense of the word, a human phenomenon, the kind of phenomenon which cannot be disregarded by anybody who is trying to discover what religion is, and what are the deep needs which it must satisfy."[5]

The empirical evidence that psychedelics such as mushrooms, iboga, ayahuasca, LSD and MDMA are effective in healing trauma is well established. They may be more effective than any other form of therapy. When taken in the context of a mutually trusting psychotherapeutic relationship, and in sacred ceremony with integrative follow-up, healing is both faster and deeper.[6] Scottish psychiatrist Dr. Ben Sessa believes that MDMA, for example, is psychiatry's antibiotic, so effective is it as an aid in healing emotional trauma. If politicians examined the evidence, as they are doing with marijuana, he believes psychedelics would be regulated and legalized.[7]

In this book I add my own healing story as empirical support to the stories of thousands of souls whose lives have been enriched, deepened and ultimately healed by these medicines.

Before I take you with me on my healing journey, I have some people to thank. I have received unconditional support from my beautiful wife, Mia. Her patience and care have been unfailing, matched only by her courage to be authentic and to challenge me when I projected ghosts from the past onto her. I would not have been able to do this without her support and am deeply grateful for her love and encouragement.

I also want to thank my therapist and mentor, Andrew Feldmar, a pioneer in the field of psychedelic psychotherapy. For over forty years he has been guiding individuals, from adolescents to octogenarians, into the depths of their souls. He neither procures nor administers these medicines. But, like a shaman, his sure and non-anxious presence holds out a lifeline for soul sojourners while they ascend and descend the ladder of life.

I wish to thank my ayahuascero, Ronin Nai, and his incredible team of dedicated souls, including Nai Niwe, Beth and Darcy. At considerable legal

---

5   Quoted in Aldous Huxley, *Doors of Perception* (New York: Harper and Brothers, 1954), 65.

6   This book is not the place to go into these peer-reviewed studies, but for an overview I refer you to the Psychedelic Bibliography on the Multidisciplinary Association for Psychedelic Studies (MAPS) website (http://www.maps.org/resources/psychedelic-bibliography).

7   "VolteFace: Is MDMA Psychiatry's Antibiotic?" on the MAPS website (http://www.maps.org/research/articles/6268-volteface-is-mdma-psychiatry's-antibiotic).

risk these beautiful people make this medicine available, presiding over ceremonies with deep wisdom, compassion and well-honed skill.

There are pioneers in this field of psychedelic research and healing, many of whom I have not met but on whose shoulders I nonetheless stand. I have read their work and been supported in my journey by their wisdom and courage. I thank psychedelic researcher and psychiatrist Stan Grof; Rick Doblin, founder of Multidisciplinary Association for Psychedelic Studies; Dr. William Richards, psychologist and leading psilocybin researcher at Johns Hopkins University; Dr. James Fadiman and Dr. Peter Levine, psychologists; mycologist Dr. Paul Stamets; psychologist Dr. Robert Firestone; and Dr. Bessel van der Kolk, trauma researcher and psychiatrist. My heartfelt gratitude for your work.

CHAPTER 1

Down the Rabbit Hole

"There's no use trying," Alice said; "one can't believe impossible things."

"I daresay you haven't had much practice," said the Queen. "When I was younger, I always did it for half an hour a day. Why, sometimes I've believed as many as six impossible things before breakfast."

— **Lewis Carroll,** ***Alice in Wonderland***

Suspending Disbelief

I'm lying on my mat in a Mexican maloca (an Amazonian communal building) with twenty-five other souls. We have each consumed an ounce of ayahuasca, a foul-tasting tea that brings on visions and takes you places you don't necessarily want to go but need to go. I have purged violently into a yogurt container. "Purging" is what an outside observer would recognize as vomiting, but it's not quite the same thing (more on this later).

When I'm finished, an intelligence is telling me to open my mouth. I'm not hearing voices. I'm silently receiving instructions. The opening is passive, as if my mouth is *being* opened.

This time it is not to purge. I am letting in the universe, swallowing it whole. Don't ask me how that's possible. Intuitively I understand that all the stars, trillions of them, are drawing from me, through some kind of electrical current, all that is not love. I receive the teaching that the stars are not inert bodies of gas and vapor, twinkling in the night sky for our enjoyment. They are living, active participants in the purification and redemption of human beings.

Uh-huh.

I know. I'm a rationalist too. Even as the medicine does its job, I'm working hard to suspend my disbelief. It sounds like something from the Twilight Zone — stars drawing from me all that is not love?

But it gets crazier. The shaman's chanting, along with the cosmic extraction of the stars, seems to be producing some kind of exorcism. I've left my body, or my body has left me. I am matterless and porous: pure energy.

The notes of the shaman's chants (sung in Shipibo, the language of the Peruvian Shipibo tribe) are transformed electrical currents. Don't ask me how I know this. I just know. The notes are entering the cells of my body. As the chant sounds, the DNA of my cells is scanned for abnormalities. I see that these abnormalities are where trauma got stuck in my body. The transformed notes, now appearing as multicoloured laser beams, seek out and find trauma in my body. When these areas are discovered, everything intensifies and deepens.

I'm now laughing to myself, wondering if people understand what the hell is going on here. It's surgery! The shaman lays his hands on one person at a time. But he's also working on everybody at once. I see that the medicine anesthetizes. We're immobilized so the surgery can proceed. I'm not sure why this doesn't freak me out. But I can sense, strange as it is, that what is happening is gracious and benevolent.

That's when it occurs to me that the shaman is channeling some kind of extra-earthly super-intelligence charged with helping humans to evolve. The ayahuasca tea is opening us up to the influence of this intelligence. Sheesh. This is my first experience of the medicine, but I damn sure didn't expect this.

Here's what's being transmitted to me: *Bruce, you need to heal your trauma. Then your spiritual evolution will take care of itself.*

I don't know what I expected when I signed up for the ceremony, but this is a surprise, to put it mildly. What trauma, exactly, do I have to heal? It will take another three years, but eventually all will be revealed.

I can't claim that what I saw and heard is true for everyone, or even true at all, except to me. I suspect that this medicine reveals itself in a thousand different ways, depending on the worldview each of us brings to the ceremony. I've written for over a decade about conscious evolution, so it makes sense that this would be one of my interpretive frameworks. But that doesn't explain the extraterrestrial details.

The next morning at the integration circle I share my experience. The shaman says, "You went deep. Be gentle with yourself. You are very open right now."

Jesus as Shaman

Jesus.

I mean, Jesus comes to mind. This isn't surprising. For twenty-eight years I contended with him, week after week, as a preacher. This discipline made me realize that he was so radical we still don't get him, in part because he's coming from Spirit and we're trying to integrate it into our everyday lives. But it's our everyday lives and everyday selves that he challenged. These lives are too small, too focused on survival to understand what he's on about. As the New Testament tells us, if you want to follow in his path it leads away from everyday life, and the everyday self, to the cross. A spiritual death is involved. Depending on the century, this might mean physical death as well.

Since the fourth century AD, however, things have changed. At that time the emperor, Constantine, selected Christianity as the empire's official religion. Ever since it has been a helpful adjunct to empire's agenda. Still today, Christianity and the state are bedfellows. Most churches, with the exception of a handful of progressive congregations, have tried desperately to fit Jesus snugly into conventional norms and values. This Jesus bears little resemblance to the historical figure.

Etymologically, "radical" means "getting down to the roots." Good people fill churches, doing good things for the world, but in my experience there is something like a force field that prevents either ascent to the pinnacle of realization or descent to the roots of what Jesus was about. Maybe it's an unconscious agreement to not take it all too seriously. Or maybe his truth has been accommodated to a culture of privilege and security that nobody, including this preacher, wanted to disrupt.

In John's gospel, Jesus teaches that we must be born again. Our firstborn lives must be shed. This doesn't happen by confessing that Jesus is Lord and Saviour. It happens when we wake up and realize that what passes for life in conventional society is actually death, and that only by dying to this life, and to the traumatized self that fell into its trance, do we find true life.

After my initial encounter with ayahuasca, I wondered if Jesus was a shaman. He acted in much the same way as the shaman, the shaman's chants and the stars worked in the ceremony. As a healer he drew from people everything that was not love. To stand in his presence was to have all the pretenses of ego exposed, every compromise with darkness and evil brought to the surface, and to be summoned to a life animated by Source, the generative, loving Matrix out of which universes arise and evolve, the Spirit at the base of all things. Like a shaman he metabolized fear, violence, envy, bitterness, darkness of all kinds and illness — everything that was not love — and raised this dark energy to a higher frequency, transforming it for the purposes of love.

The New Testament portrays him as an exorcist, casting out foreign entities that don't belong. He heals people and sometimes even brings them back from death. Liberal Christianity dismisses these stories of healing and exorcism as primitive ways of understanding what we now know better through psychology.

I don't buy it. Psychedelic medicines opened my eyes to a much more robust and complex cosmology than the one presented by scientific empiricism or liberal Christianity. At the time of the New Testament, people were not in the grip of rationalism. As powerful as reason is, when it shuts down our intuitive modes of knowing, we lose access to whole chunks of reality, and what is considered "possible" shrinks dramatically.

The further back we go in time, the more permeable we find human awareness to extraordinary dimensions of consciousness. In truth, most of reality is cut out when we conflate the totality of consciousness with rational thought. Jesus, like shamans before him, sensed and inhabited multiple levels of reality, a capacity that we have mostly lost.

Jesus enacted his shamanic role by metabolizing all the accumulated historical hatred and violence of our species, which was directed against him by the elite. He took this violence into his own body and redeemed it by returning violence and hatred with his own suffering love. Most of us do just the opposite. We unconsciously transform our suffering into violence, hatred and resentment. History thereby continues to unfold as a story of violence.

Wars, holocausts and social inequality transmit this violence, unquestionably. But what is less appreciated is that the sacred institution of the family also transmits this violence. In the privacy of families, untold violence is committed against innocent children, on a spectrum from emotional neglect to physical and sexual abuse. All this violence is the perpetuation of physical, emotional and psychological trauma passed down through families and political states from one generation to the next.

In the book of Genesis, God laments having made humans because there is so much violence in their hearts, and promptly sends a great flood. This story, versions of which are recounted in other religions, is an interpretation of a natural disaster. But it's not surprising that these early scribes understood it as a divine response to human violence — that is, to interpret a great flood as a reboot of the human species, wiping away all the violence so we could start over. Nor is it surprising that Jesus's life has similarly been interpreted as an attempt to expose, subvert and redeem regimes of violence, within and without.

Atonement Is On Us

The doctrine of atonement — in popular parlance "Jesus died for our sins" — is an attempt to redeem violence. Rather than punish humans again with another flood or similar natural disaster, the idea is that God suffers this violence on the cross. The problem with this belief is that nobody can atone for anybody else. However, Jesus may have been showing us how to do it — for ourselves! He was an example of how to participate, personally, in the redemption and evolution of our species.

What happened on the cross wasn't a once-and-for-all event. What Jesus underwent, we must undergo. The gospel story was never a story to be merely believed and then told over and over again in church — as if it all happened back there two thousand years ago, as if Jesus took care of it for us.

Instead, the gospel story describes a spiritual initiation that each individual must undergo. It was always meant to be re-enacted in each of our lives. All of us need to "go to the cross" and participate directly in the redemption of our own ancestral lineage.

In the ayahuasca ceremony, the healing I underwent was not only personal. Psychedelics brought to the surface my own repressed trauma, but I also saw that I was healing my whole ancestry by refusing to perpetuate the violence that went back millennia. I saw this history of violence and how it had flowed down to me through my family. I felt compassion (which means "to suffer with"), because I saw the big picture — not just my own suffering but that of my parents and their parents and their parents, etc.

My journey for the next few years was about integrating all of this. It's one thing to understand it spiritually, but my psyche (my essential and unique character) and my body needed time to catch up. I sensed that I was being recruited to a life of love, to be a co-redeemer with all these courageous spiritual warriors willing to do their part in putting an end to the violence in their own ancestry.

CHAPTER 2

Bone on Bone

To live in this world
you must be able
to do three things:
to love what is mortal;
to hold it
against your bones knowing
your own life depends on it;
and, when the time comes
to let it go,
to let it go.

— Mary Oliver, "In Blackwater Woods"

Blessed Breath

I've just taken 120 milligrams of MDMA and 300 micrograms of LSD. My therapist is holding me, my head resting on his shoulder, his hand cupping my head tenderly. I've been working with him for over two years at this point.

I am breathing deeply, more deeply than I remember ever breathing. There is only breath, moving through the entire length and breadth of my body. No thoughts. It feels good. God, it feels good to breathe, just breathe.

So this is what it feels like to trust. Before the great betrayal, before the unimaginable possibility that I wasn't welcome in the world, there exists this state of trust. Trust is innocence. Deep breathing is what a body does when it has no reason to question the goodness of life, the benevolence of the other. This breathing is embodied trust.

No thoughts. No worries. No plans. No me. I am breath. I am being breathed. It's freaky how much whatever is breathing me wants to just breathe. It's like a lifetime of not breathing is getting healed. I feel like a human bellows. It is effortless.

A thought arises:

So this is how it works. Source lives through my breathing. All those yoga classes that start with breathing: I never got what all the fuss was about. The teacher speaks of pranayama, *the life force found in our breath. Google it and most sources will tell you it means "control of the breath." That's exactly what doesn't need to happen. "Releasing the body from distrust so that it can be breathed by Source" is more like it. I've controlled my breath for too many decades. All I want to do is breathe like this for the rest of my life.*

To the Bone

I take my therapist's collarbone between my thumb and index finger. It feels, well, real — more real and more reality than I've ever let in. I run my thumb and index finger along the full length of the bone. My touch is welcome. This is such a relief that tears come to my eyes.

This feeling of reality grows in intensity. Feeling me feeling his bones he says, "Never mind flesh on flesh. Try bone on bone!" His voice is deep and gravelly, capturing the depth of the moment.

"Bone on bone."

Bones are about as close to the earth as we will ever get as incarnated souls. I learned early to travel north, away from my body, towards discarnate ideas and ideals of how I should be, if I wanted to survive.

But here I am, touching the living skeleton of my therapist. It feels like touching him, his essence. He feels it too. Ancient shamanism, along with other religions, taught that bones held our essential nature and memory. They continued to be animated by the soul of the animal or the saint after death. Skeletons represent the enduring truth because they outlast the outer layer of flesh. If we get down to the "bare bones of a situation," we are getting to the truth concealed by attempts to obfuscate.

We speak of knowing something "in our bones" when the knowing transcends intellectual knowledge. Bone-deep knowing can't be taught. It must be felt.

The collarbone, or clavicle, is the most vulnerable bone in the body. It is distinctive in that muscle surrounds most bones in the body but not the collarbone. Without this muscle, it is one of the easiest bones to break. At birth, it is not uncommon for babies to break a collarbone during delivery.

As I touch my therapist's collarbone, I feel as though I am accessing the vulnerability of the human condition. And that vulnerability is the key to being human.

The Story of the Bone Flute

There is a Grimm Brothers fairy tale concerning two brothers. The elder had evil in his heart, and the younger was innocent and good-hearted. The kingdom was under siege by a monstrous boar living deep in the forest. Desperate, the king offered the hand of his daughter in marriage to whoever would slay it. The brothers were very poor farmers, and the prospect of becoming royalty appealed to them. They set out from opposite ends of the forest.

The younger brother came upon one of the small persons of the forest, who gave him a spear. The older brother partied with some friends rather than setting out immediately. Sure enough, the younger brother came upon the monstrous boar. He held his spear out, piercing its heart and killing the animal. As he carried the boar back home, he came upon his older brother, still enjoying the revelry. When the older brother saw the boar, he was envious.

The next day he asked his younger brother to show him the place in the forest where he killed the boar. Halfway through the forest they crossed a bridge that carried travelers over a raging river far below. The older brother came up from behind and pushed his brother into the river, drowning him. The older brother presented the boar to the king and married the king's daughter.

Many years later, a shepherd found a bone by the riverside. He thought he would carve a flute from this bone. When he finished, he played the instrument. The sound that came out was the voice of the younger brother telling the story of what happened to him. The shepherd traveled to the king and played the whole story on the flute, exposing the older brother's evil act. The king had the older brother put death.

This story captures my experience of working with psychedelic medicine. The medicine takes us bone-deep into the true story of our life. It tells the story of the forgotten trauma, the unutterable and forgotten crime that shaped so much of our lives. Healing happens when our true song is played and witnessed. This is what happens in psychedelic psychotherapy. This song of our life, including the unspoken violence we suffered, needs to be heard and witnessed if we are to heal.

The psychotherapist plays the role of the shepherd. In her hands the dead and buried memories of pain and betrayal are played back to us and witnessed. The bare-bones story of our life is revealed. Our bone-deep story is hard to get at because, like the murder of the younger brother, our betrayal occurred in the context and secrecy of our own family. We dissociate from this story and deny it because it is too painful.

There is an inherent intensity and intimacy to life, like feeling a living bone between the bones of my thumb and index finger. This is lost in response to trauma and regained when the shepherd plays the bone flute.

Bone on bone. I am! You are. I exist and so do you. Even though we will remain forever a mystery to each other, yet I know, in my bones, that I am through you, and you are through me. I can't get over the miracle of our existing and being together. It's so simple, but if it's so simple, why do I live most of my life apart from the mystery?

CHAPTER 3

Trauma: Falling from Grace

The past is never dead. It's not even past.
— William Faulkner, *Requiem for a Nun*

Hijacked

In the same LSD session, my easy breathing suddenly becomes shallow. I am anxious.

Why am I afraid to be more alive than I've ever felt? It's what I want. I am in a state of trust, finally. This is what I've been waiting for all my life.

At least it's what I *say* I want. In this moment of increased intimacy and intensity I've stepped across a threshold into foreign territory. In this space of super-consciousness I watch myself pull away from all the good feelings of intimate connection. How often have I pulled away like this in my life?

The medicine has removed my well-honed defenses. I sit up and straddle my willing therapist, who is still lying down. He asks, "What's going on?"

"Do you enjoy this?" I ask him.

What I mean is, do you really want to be here, or are you here because I pay you? And beneath this question is the mother lode: *Do you love me?*

Do I belong? I'm excruciatingly vulnerable. How can I trust that you want to be with me? Not just because I'm paying you but because you love me.

It is a familiar feeling, born of insecurity about whether I belong in this world. We either acquire this sense of being welcome in the world very early in life, or we don't. Hell is never being sure. This insecurity means the difference between proceeding with confidence in life or chronically testing the waters, like a puppy's first experience of the ocean. Am I in or out? Do you love me, or are you going to hurt me?

So here I am, here we are. I'm afraid that my therapist does not want to be with me. He assures me that he is not a prostitute. I laugh. It's a relief to witness my insecurity being played out so directly. Too much of my life has been an unconscious reenactment of this deep insecurity.

I now understand why, when I show up at events, I feel a moment of doubt about whether I have the right time and place. I am bracing for rejection, trying to protect myself from the shame of discovering that I am uninvited and unwanted. This is the past hijacking the present.

The power of the medicine is that I know intuitively what's going on. I don't need a therapist to interpret it for me. I know where my question is coming from, as does he. He smiles and asks, "Why don't you enjoy this moment?" This is a serious question meant to inspire contemplation, not shame. He is wise enough not to interpret what's happening. I have no reason to question whether he wants to be with me. For the past two years he's done nothing but support me. This question doesn't belong to this moment. It belongs to the past.

But I can't enjoy the moment of connection because I received feedback early in life that my mother didn't *truly* want to connect with me. My attachment with her was insecure; it was interrupted repeatedly before I was ready. Such disruptions are shocking and heartbreaking to an infant or toddler.

We underestimate the intuitive intelligence of children. From a very early age we know the truth about whether our mothers and fathers are available for secure connection. If the truth we discover is that they are not available, we start compensating. This compensation takes us further and further away from our natural, essential nature. It will haunt us for a lifetime until we bring it to consciousness.

Why don't you enjoy this moment?

My therapist's simple question contains everything. Why don't I simply enjoy my life? Why the chronic rumination? Why the vigilance? Why the shallow breathing? Why the pervasive skepticism and cynicism? Why tolerate not being comfortable? Why the lack of self-respect? Why the dark moods? Why the rage? Why is connecting and staying connected in intimate relationships so challenging?

Much spiritual teaching these days emphasizes being "present" and in the "now." Which is great advice. But it's not great advice when dealing with trauma. When it comes to trauma, "being here, now" is actually hell. The parts of the brain associated with the sense of linear time — of having a past, present and future — go offline. We carry our past with us into every moment of our life, and for most of us our past is full of unconscious (repressed) trauma. Telling people to "be here, now" is of limited value if those people believe in their hearts, albeit unconsciously, that being here, now means being shamed, mistreated or extinguished. Hopelessness arises. Only when we can tell a different story, with an outcome different from the trauma memory, are we able to heal.

Imagination is at the core of the human experience. Psychologist Joan Borysenko teaches participants in her workshops to take a trauma experience that is yet unresolved and to give it a "hero's ending" — one in which the hero successfully slays the metaphorical dragon. The brain doesn't actually know the difference between reality and fantasy, so the imagined narrative with a new ending can rewire the brain.

Trauma as Failure of Love

"Trauma," as I'm using the term, refers to failures of love in early childhood. The common tendency is to associate trauma exclusively with war veterans, holocaust survivors, torture victims and others, generally adults, who have been through horrific experiences. Of course, these are all occasions of unspeakable trauma. But in my experience the shock of discovering that those who were supposed to love us failed is likewise traumatic, and can have lifelong consequences. These failures of love are forgotten or repressed, but our lives become their living artifact.

The body, nervous system and brain don't distinguish between types of trauma. Once triggered, the autonomic nervous system releases hormones to help us be in flight or fight mode, or to freeze. To the brain and hormonal system, failures of love, whether caused by lack of attention, shaming, neglect, physical or sexual abuse, are the same as being bombed.

Leading trauma expert Bessel van der Kolk has come to a sobering realization:

> This is why trauma that has occurred within relationships is generally more difficult to treat than trauma resulting from traffic accidents or natural disasters. In our society the most common traumas in women and children occur at the hands of their parents or intimate partners. Child abuse, molestation, and domestic violence are all inflicted by people who are supposed to love you. That knocks out the most important protection against being traumatized: being sheltered by the people you love.[8]

These failures require us to adapt by using our life force for survival rather than living creatively. When my therapist was being present and caring, I saw threat where there was none. I interrupted my enjoyment of the moment out of habit to defend against something that happened in the distant past.

Bessel van der Kolk points out that trauma is not remembered so much as it is relived.

Denial and Repression

Defining trauma as a failure of love was a gift of ayahuasca, which allowed me to see the impact of emotional neglect and physical punishment in my own life (see Chapter 4).

These failures of love are so pervasive and common in society that we've lowered our standard for what it means to be human. We walk around mostly unaware that our behavior and interactions are conditioned by childhood trauma and by the false persona we created to survive. We be-

---

8   Bessel van der Kolk, *The Body Keeps Score: Brain, Mind and Body in the Healing of Trauma* (New York: Penguin Books, 2014), 210.

lieve that we're free and that our interpretations of and reactions to circumstances, events and relationships are unencumbered. But in fact we are programmed by trauma, our responses to people and events dictated by the ways we learned to compensate for trauma in the past. We will never be free until we heal, but because of repression and denial we don't even realize we need to heal.

My shaman estimates that 70 percent of those who participate in the healing ceremonies with ayahuasca discover during the ceremony that they were sexually abused in childhood, and 100 percent contend with emotional abuse. Maybe the population that attends these ceremonies is skewed. They have, after all self-selected to attend a healing ceremony. But even after we've accounted for this, the extent to which trauma impacts our personal and collective lives is vastly underestimated. When the Centers for Disease Control and Kaiser Permanente studied the prevalence of "adverse childhood experiences" or ACEs (see Introduction), nearly two-thirds of the 17,000 people in their study reported experiencing at least one ACE. But the number of people who have experienced physical, emotional and sexual abuse, along with neglect, as children is probably even higher, because typically people don't remember these events without a lot of help. We don't remember because it is too painful to remember and because denial and repression are so powerful.

It Never "Just Happens"

When I come down off the medicine, I watch myself instinctively make excuses for what happened and downplay the impact of this trauma. It's right there in the way I wrote that last sentence. "What happened" suggests that something just accidentally and passively occurred. But the truth, as my therapist points out, is that when it comes to trauma, somebody actively did something to someone else. It's an ethical failure, and the most difficult thing to face is that the "somebody" was the same person (or people) that my life depended on. My default language conveys the power of denial and repression.

When we are young and vulnerable, we cannot accept that we are not loved. We can't even understand that fact, let alone integrate it into our worldview. Our survival depends on being loved, so we do whatever we have to do to be loved.

With the help of the medicine, I remembered how, as a toddler, I interpreted both the threat and enactment of physical violence against me: "She will kill me if I don't do what she wants." Was it true or not? Would she (my mother) really have killed me? To a small child it is true. To my nervous system it is true. To my mind, which would shape future core beliefs, it was true. What I saw was a giant mercilessly coming at me.

The impact of this belief lasts a lifetime. It did for me. Whenever I was called to stand up for myself, express a viewpoint that differed from the majority stand, establish a boundary, challenge an authority, express my uniqueness or negotiate for what I wanted, if it challenged another person, this belief operated in the background. *I might be killed if I don't do what the other wants.*

To make matters worse, I was a "spiritual" leader. This meant that I was rewarded in the eyes of others for acquiescing. Acquiescence was called "humility" or non-attachment or some other spiritual bullshit. But it wasn't that at all. "Humble acquiescence" was in fact an unconscious fear of being killed if I didn't do what the other wanted.

I watch how my mind, even in the ceremony, justifies the violence. I defend my mother to maintain the fantasy that I was loved. "It wasn't so bad," I tell myself. "Others had it worse than me. She must have been so overwhelmed by my need." I develop what psychologist Robert Firestone calls the "fantasy bond," making up a story that I was being loved when I wasn't, and then defending that story, along with my mother, with every ounce of resolve I possess.

But in the midst of this denial I see the words FAILURE TO LOVE. written across the screen of my consciousness. The period in that sentence is particularly emphasized: Failure to love. Period. I am being asked to face this straight up.

Love makes us feel that we matter, that we are of consequence and that the universe is for us. Love means emotional attunement (that is, somebody is aware of how you feel, is reading your moods and thoughts, and is responding accordingly). Love means that somebody is meeting our needs and wants without resentment — even with joy. Love means that somebody is signaling that we are an absolute delight. Love means being known and being gently drawn, with authentic curiosity, toward our fullest expression.

Without this love from outside, we do not learn how to love ourselves, respect ourselves or treat ourselves with dignity. Nor do we learn how to stop others when they mistreat us. Trauma inculcates the fallacy of passivity, teaching us that there is nothing to be done and that there is nothing that *can* be done. This mistreatment, we come to believe, is just how life works. The defeatist attitude stems from a memory of a time when this was literally true, when we were so small that there truly was nothing we could do. But when we act as if this is true when we are adults, it's the past hijacking the present, outside our awareness.

Guardians of the Threshold

It is not always *mistreatment* that makes us anxious. We come to expect mistreatment if we've been traumatized. It barely registers. Rather, the moment somebody treats us with tenderness and kindness we become anxious and reject the person and the treatment. If we didn't reject them, we might get emotional. Maybe we'd bawl our eyes out, without having a clue why. The bulwark we built against the flood of grief would come crashing down, and we'd be carried away in its torrent — back down the river of our life to the source of our grief.

Mythologist Joseph Campbell identifies the three stages of the myth of the hero: leaving home, ordeal and rebirth, returning home a new person. After the hero has left home, the realm of the known and the familiar, she encounters "the guardians of the threshold." Beyond these guardians awaits the unknown, the Un-self, the adventure that will require a psychological and spiritual death. The guardians are there to warn and protect. "Go beyond this threshold," they warn, "and you will surely die." Once the hero steps into this territory (that is, once she has crossed the threshold) there is no going back.

For some people, an innocent but genuine compliment can trigger an encounter with the guardians of our threshold. The compliment signals that you matter, you are worthy and you just might have something important to contribute. All good, right? But no, it's not so simple.

Early in our lives, in the absence of love, we set the bar low, expecting to receive minimal scraps of attention and affection. Subsequent gestures of kindness, tenderness and respect from others bring in levels of love that easily surpass the threshold we have set and summon the guardians of our psyche. These are instinctual reactions, built into our blood, bones and nervous system, that are meant to protect us from feeling the heartbreak of failures of love. This heartbreak was simply too painful when we were little, so we constructed a fortress around our heart, and a personality to go with it, to buffer us against re-experiencing the original devastation.

This is why birthday celebrations, work compliments, sports achievements and other events that make us the center of attention can evoke anxiety. We don't feel worthy of the attention. All the fuss takes us out of our comfort zone. If I let a celebration or compliment register in my bones, a whole Pandora's box will open. Feelings associated with past failures of love will be released. The whole house of cards that is the personality I constructed to cope with trauma and keep it at bay might come crashing down. Better to deflect praise than allow it to be a wrecking ball.

A psychotherapeutic journey, with or without psychedelics, is a hero's journey. You will go places that you do not want to go. You will discover your thresholds and your guardians. But you may also discover, as I have, what it means to be "twice born." Freedom, the capacity to make choices that are based in the present and not in past fears and failures of love, is at stake. So is love. Not until we can bring to consciousness all the failures of love will we be able to feel again our longing for love and to cross the threshold into new regions of intimacy.

CHAPTER 4

The False Self

The false self is for survival. The true self is for life.

— **Andrew Feldmár**

The Ceremony and the Tea

I'm lying prostrate in a room with twenty-five other souls who are crossing the threshold. It's pitch dark, the room lit only by the occasional flare of Bic lighters. Before the ceremony we are each smudged with braided sweetgrass, used for millennia by indigenous people for purification. The shaman then blows mapacho smoke over us. Mapacho is a wild tobacco used for spiritual cleansing, to "bring on" the medicine, and to reorient participants after a challenging experience. The veterans among us are smoking mapacho in pipes and perfuming themselves with agua de Florida, an American version of a sweet Peruvian citrus cologne that is believed to attract plant spirits. The shaman will also put a small amount of this in his mouth and then spray it on the recipient out of his mouth in an attempt to clear the energy field. Together, these elements create portals into other realms, worlds above, below and within. A few participants are moaning, others quietly weeping. And some are, well, puking into plastic yogurt containers — the receptacle of choice for these ceremonies.

My shaman and his assistant are chanting. He's been singing these chants, along with songs of the Lakota people, for the past four hours and will continue for another two hours.

We are over halfway into an ayahuasca ceremony. Four hours ago, each of us approached the shaman and knelt before him as he measured out a shot glass full of the tea. This is a sober moment, filled with equal measures of anticipation and apprehension. We've all decided to let go of our tight grip on reality.

Mystery shrouds the tea's origin. Shamans make the potent brew by combining the leaves of *Psychotria viridis* and the vine of *Banisteriopsis caapi,* but the chances of someone stumbling upon this recipe by trial and error are minuscule. The combination came to shamans in dreams. This only seems far-fetched to us because we've lost access to this way of listening to the intelligence of plants in the modern world.

When the Life We're Living Is Not Our Own

I'm now four hours into the ayahuasca ceremony. After being shown how I was hurt as a child, a cascading series of insights fall on me. It's like it's all revealed at once, but I require the dimension of time to integrate what's happening. In bold letters, written across the screen of my consciousness are these words:

MY LIFE HAS NOT BEEN MY OWN

I wander out of the maloca and gaze up at the stars. I repeat again and again, "Fuck me. Fuck me."

The assistant comes out. We're not supposed to talk, but I have to tell somebody. "My life has not been my own," I whisper.

I'm fifty-nine and I'm just seeing this now, thanks to the medicine. "Fuck me." I cannot get over it. And then I see how I constructed my personality in response to trauma — a personality underneath which my true self lay hidden away.

Without any drama, and maybe tinged with the humor of someone who has seen it all, the assistant offers, "You'll get over it."

The sad thing is, as psychiatrist Alice Miller puts it, when the false self is revealed, it isn't necessarily a homecoming. This is because there was no home. It's a *discovery* of home.

I first came across the term "false self" over twenty years ago when I read Miller's book *The Drama of the Gifted Child*. The false self is the self we develop to survive. It's not exactly "false" though. We construct it in response to specific, shitty, life conditions. We adapt to survive. In this sense, it's a highly intelligent response. When conditions are threatening, emotionally or physically, we must pay close attention to what is expected of us — or else. We can no longer trust spontaneous, relaxed behavior, because this elicited punishment and shame. We acquire a habit of vigilance as we scan the environment for cues. This habit lasts a lifetime.

We may intuitively realize, as I did, that love is not on offer. In response, I asked: What do I need to do to be *liked* then? As in, not destroyed. I'll be good. I'll be caring. I'll be sensitive. I'll be small. I'll be big. I'll be entertaining. I'll be quiet. I won't need you. I'll take care of you.

We trade our natural, spontaneous, relational self for an unnatural, constrained, lonely self in the interests of survival. As we age, we forget that we ever had any other way of being in the world. We proceed as though our life is a performance in someone else's drama. We carry this into our intimate relationships, treating lovers like they are the directors of our life.

For example, as mentioned, I formed a belief, at a very early age, that my mother was willing to kill me if I didn't do what she wanted. This belief was formed in response to being physically hit when she was enraged. So I learned to be "good," to be quiet, to not demand anything. I'm told that, in the beginning, I protested. But a toddler will never win this battle, and eventually I collapsed in the face of overwhelming odds. This early defeat wired me to develop an acute sensitivity to what women want from me — forgetting, because I never really knew, that what women want is for men to show up and fight for what they want.

When we feel frightened as children, we end up, as did I, parenting the parent. We become attuned to the needs of the parent and ask, "What do you need me to be for you to be happy?" The first order of business is making the parent happy, because if mother isn't happy, she can't take care of us, her children, and we won't survive. It's not altruistic. It's taking care of our own needs. But as adults, if we proceed from this unconscious motivation, it can *seem* altruistic. Actually, it's learned cowardice.

This is why parents need to get this stuff sorted out before having children. If we haven't consciously integrated our own trauma, we come to the rigorous task of parenting with a barrel full of unmet needs. And we expect our children to meet them. We don't expect this consciously. But unconsciously a child's cry may trigger, not empathy, but deep frustration and anger that is related less to the present-day situation than it is to how our own cries were punished when we were children. Tenderness is not an option if we were punished for crying.

We adapt in a million different subtle and not-so-subtle ways. I became a pleaser, not wanting to risk the wrath of my mother. I learned to repress my own needs and wants and to become very attuned to hers. Which is not what childhood is for.

The thing about the false self is that it doesn't just go away one day all by itself. It takes over your personality. And you can spend a lifetime thinking it's the real you. But it's not. It's the "you" that was under siege. It's more than a little tragic. I spent too many decades blissfully ignorant that I was living through, or behind, this frightened self.

I came across the following piece, which the American novelist F. Scott Fitzgerald wrote near the end of his life. He was experiencing monumental failure after great success early in his career: "I had weaned myself from all the things I used to love — that every act of life, from the morning toothbrush to the friend at dinner had become an effort. I saw that for a long time I had not liked people and things, but only followed the rickety old pretence of liking. I saw that even my love for those closest to me had become only an attempt to love, that my casual relations — with an editor, a tobacco seller, the child of a friend, were only what I remembered I *should* do, from other days."[9]

There are many ways to interpret the cause of Fitzgerald's ennui. I hear in his words a man who had lost himself, but not because of his growing unpopularity. His "pretence" of liking people and things, and his discovery

---

9   F. Scott Fitzgerald, "The Crack-Up," *Esquire*, March 7, 2017, available on the *Esquire* website (https://www.esquire.com/lifestyle/a4310/the-crack-up/).

that his "attempt to love" was motivated by mere social pressure and memory, is a clear description of a man who had been living someone else's life through his adapted, or false, self.

If this sounds familiar, the good news is that there are aspects of the false self that can serve us well. When we become conscious of what's happened, we can relegate the false self to the back seat, ready when needed to take directions from our true self. There are all kinds of competencies that we can recruit when needed. The goal is to do this consciously. For example, I became very good at tuning in the feelings of others. This is handy as a therapist, but it's tyrannical when it's merely an unconscious scanning to make sure I'm safe. Over time I have learned to distinguish genuine threats in the present from past trauma. Perhaps more importantly, I am more compassionate with myself whether the threat belongs to the present or the past. I am free to remove myself from the situation rather than endure it.

Mommy's Little Hero

The medicine shines a powerful light on how we compensate for these failures of love. I see how I constructed my false self. In a ceremony I came up with a name for this self: *Mommy's Little Hero.* His inner voice seems proud and strong, but underneath is a frightened little boy: *The rest of my siblings might bother you with their needs and wants, but not me. I know that you are overwhelmed and I'll take care of you by not asking for anything. See? I can take care of myself. I am strong.*

How often do you hear somebody responding to an offer of help with the words, "No, I'm good" —

> meaning, I don't want to be a burden —
> meaning, I can't risk being a burden because you can't handle it —
> meaning, You might destroy me.

However, all this self-negation happens outside awareness. Case in point: I carried in the groceries the other day. I had the bag under my arm, with a cup of tea in one hand and my leashed dog, Koa, in the other. I arrived at the front door with my wife, empty-handed, beside me. Rather than ask if she could open the door for me, I actually tried to do it myself. I can laugh at it now, but you get the idea.

When my first marriage was in trouble, we went to a marriage therapist. He asked us both to state ten things we needed from the other. My former wife breezed through her list. Then he turned to me. I swear, I couldn't find a single thing I needed from her. Which is just weird. And sad. Not to mention that this made my former wife feel like she was of zero consequence.

Self-Mothering

Psychologist Robert Firestone tells the story of working with a catatonic man. He presented the man with a glass of milk and a glass of the patient's own urine. When asked what came out of his penis, the man told his therapist that it was milk. When asked to choose between the two glasses, he always chose the "milk" that came out of his own penis. Firestone cites this story as an example of behavior that stems from a refusal to need anything from another human being. Better to keep the fantasy of self-sufficiency alive at all costs than risk trusting another human. The day the patient chose fresh milk over urine was the day Firestone knew he was making progress. The real milk represented dependence on the mother and, by extension, his therapist. By taking it, the man was signaling his readiness to trust another human being.

Firestone called the hyper-individualism displayed by the patient choosing his urine "self-mothering." When we are children and it becomes too frightening to reach out and ask for what we need, and when we repeatedly discover our dependence is resented, we turn inward to get our needs met. Eventually we may end up a wandering nomad on an inner-city street, having animated conversations with ourselves. We are the only person we can trust, even in a conversation.

In my case, I realized that I never actually stopped needing other people. It's just that it went underground. It leaked out. People still did stuff for me, but they just picked up on my needs and took care of them. I had become sneaky enough that I never had to ask for help and thus never had to risk rejection. Which is tiresome and manipulative. But more, if we can't acknowledge our need of others and reach out for support, then neither can we be grateful. We don't even notice that the world is supporting us. We live with the fantasy that we are self-sufficient.

I'm seeing all of this clearly as I lie back in the grass outside the maloca. It's a warm summer night, and the stars have befriended me. They are winking at me. *We've been here the whole time for you, Bruce. You just needed to ask. Welcome home.*

I say out loud, "No more. It's over. No more Mommy's Little Hero. That ends now."

And then, out of nowhere, comes laughter. Comedy and tragedy are very closely related. I laugh in part because it's a relief that I've finally seen it. I have, God willing, a few decades left to be myself, spontaneous, full of my own desires, free. In part, I'm laughing at the absurdity of the human condition.

The Robot

There is one expression of the false self that I want to draw particular attention to. This is the passive self that feels bullied by life and can only *react* to changing conditions but can't *respond* creatively.

The writer who is most uncompromising about this aspect of the false self is G. I. Gurdjieff, a teacher of esoteric wisdom and psychology. He contended that humans are nothing but machines, or robots, until we wake up. We have zero freedom. Our lives, when we are asleep, are totally contingent on external conditions and circumstances. If the sun is out, we are happy. When it clouds over, we're sad. If we receive a compliment, we feel good. If somebody criticizes us, we are morose. If we achieve a goal, we want to celebrate. If we don't succeed, a terrible mood overcomes us. We are like "reeds blown in the wind," to quote John the Baptist describing those whose lives are determined by changing circumstances.

In this metaphor, the wind is every external influence that makes us feel as though life just "happens" to us. We are passive victims of changing circumstances. What is necessary is to be able to "do" — that is, to act with freedom. But we don't act because we haven't yet admitted that we are helpless machines. War will never cease, says Gurdjieff, because we are automatons that believe we are free. Geopolitical circumstances cause the war, we tell ourselves, not us, not human beings.

The analogy he uses to describe human beings in this state where everything just "happens" to us is the horse-drawn carriage. Humans have four "bodies." The first body is the physical body, the equivalent of the carriage. The second body, the horse, comprises feelings and desires. The third body is the mind or intellect. This is the driver. The fourth body is consciousness, the true "I," who is the master.

In Gurdjieff's view, the human machine takes its cues from the first body, which is totally determined by external circumstances. This body (the carriage) then controls the second body (the horse), determining what it desires and feels. In turn, both the first and second bodies control our third body (thoughts). So our thoughts (the driver) are taking cues from the horse and carriage. This is literally putting the cart before the horse, and the driver! The fourth body, the master and only unified and coherent "I," is nowhere to be seen in this arrangement. The first three bodies each believe that they are the true "I," in charge of the others. This is the divided self of the human machine.

You may notice that this arrangement is precisely the story that materialistic science tells. The human is little more than a machine run by genetic material, firing neurons, biochemistry, the gray matter of the brain, social circumstances, etc. This machine is absolutely determined by a universe that obeys purely physical and accidental laws. There is no freedom.

This self, says Gurdjieff, is not even a self. It's a whole bunch of imposters pretending to be singular and free, and taking great offense should somebody suggest otherwise. But if we do our work, which is to become self-aware, we may realize freedom. This requires first a total acceptance that we are imprisoned and that our main task as humans is to break out.

If we are successful in our work, the spiritual self (the master or fourth body) develops a unified will. He then gives orders to the intellect (the driver), who in turn directs the horse, who pulls the carriage, aligned with the highest will.

The self that I was purging in ceremonies was this machine self, which is an aspect of the false self. The false self is mechanical because it can do nothing except react to, and be determined by, external influences. There is no self-mastery because there is no true self. There can be no realization of purpose because our purpose will always be driven by false motivations, such as the unconscious need for the love, acceptance and belonging that were never given to us in our formative years.

Gurdjieff doesn't delve into the impact of trauma, but my sense is that we do indeed become machines (or as literary critic and amateur psychologist Colin Wilson calls it, "robots") in response to trauma. When we learn from our parents that our natural, spontaneous and free self is not acceptable or loveable, we turn ourselves into what they need us to be. In the process we sacrifice our humanity.

The Passive Self

The other expression of the false self that is related to, but distinguishable from, the machine self is the passive self. This is the self that feels bullied by reality and has concluded that there is nothing to be done about it. The passive self manifests as a victim of life. And indeed, the child whose false self this is once was a victim, helplessly and passively enduring emotional, sexual or physical abuse. This state of passivity follows the child into adulthood. Much of therapy is about awakening agency in the traumatized individual.

I recall a dream I had immediately following an ayahuasca ceremony. I'm transported with a group of people into the future. We are operating under cover, hunted down by the secret police of that future society. I'm on a merry-go-round as I try to hide.

The scene shifts to a fancy ballroom in a luxurious palace. My body has changed. I'm very supple (which is certainly not true in reality). I'm floating through space. A crabby man appears, complaining about literally everything. The more he complains, the more the elements of his life change for the worse. He's in freezing cold water. It's gray and bleak. I'm screaming at him, trying to let him know that he's doing this to himself. His complaints are creating his reality. But he's not listening.

My wife realizes that she's pregnant. We know intuitively that it's a boy. She gets bigger and bigger. Then she starts to worry. I know that her worrying is going to create the conditions that justify her worry. Sure enough, she falls down the stairs. In the dream I realize that I am being taught about the law of manifestation: Live today as though it is the future you intend. Today *is* the future, except that in this time-bound dimension it takes time to manifest.

Then I see a warehouse full of scaffolding that is about to fall down. When it does, the nuts and bolts are scattered everywhere. I go to pick them up but am warned that this is forbidden. I am told to throw them back.

In this dream I am being taught about the "nuts and bolts" of consciousness. I am shown that I am responsible for the world I see and bring forth. The scaffolding of my old consciousness has crumbled, and I am told that I cannot take any of this old scaffolding with me — the nuts and bolts belong to an old, passive and traumatized consciousness. When this old consciousness is active, it's like being on a merry-go-round. Round and round I go, creating the same (traumatized) circumstances every single day.

This dream exposes the myth of passive consciousness, showing me that my thoughts and beliefs bring forth a corresponding reality. If my thoughts are negative, my reality will be equally negative. If they are positive, and if I believe that I can accomplish what I set my mind to, my potential is limitless. The dream shows that it is time for me to take responsibility for the world I am creating. This requires a death to that old self and the old consciousness that believes life is just happening to me and which bullies me into submission.

An interesting feature of my dream is that I am part of a group that is learning about the nature of consciousness. A faction of secret police is hunting us down. They do not want us to awaken from the dream of passivity. Films like *The Manchurian Candidate,* the Bourne trilogy and *The Matrix* externalize this faction. But my sense is that the secret police are an aspect of my own psyche, invested in keeping me passive — for fear I will cross the threshold.

The passive self is supported by the prevailing bias of modern materialistic philosophy and science that tries to persuade us consciousness is passive. The belief is that consciousness acts as a mirror, reflecting the world to us just as it is. This is the basis of scientific objectivity: The world holds still while we, controlling for subjective bias, objectively examine it. Quantum physics showed us that it's not so simple. The observer changes what is being observed in the act of observing. However, the false bifurcation of reality into observed and observer persists. This "subject–object split" has been around since René Descartes first wrote about it ("I think, therefore I am").

The philosopher Edmund Husserl, founder of phenomenology, calls this belief that consciousness is like a mirror, passively reflecting the world, the "natural standpoint." The world strikes the senses and it's up to us to interpret or misinterpret it. But consciousness is active according to Husserl. It goes out of us and grasps the world.

Mathematician and philosopher A. N. Whitehead called this "going out" of consciousness "prehension." We send consciousness out of us like an eight-armed octopus, gathering our disparate sensations and perceptions into a unity, ordering the chaos. In this way the universe organizes into more complex wholes — through our own agency!

If this is true, then our consciousness doesn't merely *reflect* a world. It participates in creating it. It's not that things don't have independent existence, or that we literally create the world. Rather, what we see is a function of the quality of an active consciousness.

Two people can look out at the world and come to completely different conclusions about it. One sees a world that is flat, colourless and without purpose. The other sees a world of exquisite beauty and meaning. It's the same world, seen through different lenses: One is the lens of a passive and depressed self who projects his inner state onto the world, while the other lens belongs to an active and vital self who projects his buoyancy and joie de vivre on the world.

The more active and vital our consciousness, the more of the world we see, the greater our powers of organization and the more complexity we can gather into a whole. This active gathering of bits of reality into wholes by consciousness makes us humans rather than machines.

The modern mind — that is, the mind that has been overtaken by the verbal-intellectual capacity — has lost access to the intuitive and imaginative faculties that science associates with the right brain. When we identify the self exclusively with the rational, left, brain, reality is divided up into its distinct, separate units that science can measure and catalog — to our benefit. But the downside is that we see with what Whitehead called "immediacy perception." That means we only see things up close, in bits and pieces. When our consciousness expands to include the intuitive, artistic and poetic side, we gain access to what he called "meaning perception." Suddenly an intricately patterned whole comes into view, what social scientist and linguist Gregory Bateson called "the pattern that connects."

Think of those pointillist paintings by Georges Seurat. View one of them up close and all you see are dabs of disconnected colour. This is immediacy perception. But step back and these thousands of discrete points form a beautiful landscape or the scene of a picnic — meaning perception. The picnic, with characters strolling blissfully through the landscape, was always there in all its beauty but we missed it because we were too close to the painting. All mystics have access to the totality of consciousness, both immediacy *and* meaning perception.

It is as if we were told that the only way to see the world is through a tiny peephole in the fence, says Colin Wilson. But the mystics stood up and looked *over* the fence. Trauma keeps us looking through the peephole at an awful world that we feel powerless to change.

Remember, the false self is a victimized self. It learned helplessness in response to early trauma. The myth of passive consciousness — that we are bullied by life — serves to reinforce the structure of the false self. It relieves us of having to take responsibility for life *as it is* today.

Self-Indulgence or Social Justice?

Why, I ask myself, is it so difficult to be tender and kind with each other, with our own children?

The answer is clear. Unredeemed trauma. Generation after generation of children inherits the violence of their ancestors. As the saying goes, hurt people hurt people. More accurately, hurt people who are unconscious of their hurt, hurt people.

I feel deep respect for my co-sojourners in the maloca. Each one is taking part in the redemption of the violence of their ancestral lineage. Some people make the claim that all this therapeutic work, and work with psychedelics, is self-indulgent. Nothing could be further from the truth. This is social justice in action. We are ridding ourselves of the violence enacted on us by those who were charged to love us. The greatest gift we can give to the human species, and to our planet, devastated by thousands of years of intergenerational trauma, is our true self. The only way to ensure we are offering our true self, not the false self, is to examine and heal our broken-heartedness. This is a truly heroic gesture, as it means we are doing our part to ensure that the violence stops with us and that future generations will grow up expressing their radiant, unique selves.

When the false self gives way, there is a resurgence of vitality. Maybe not right away, because it takes time for the true self to come out. But eventually all the energy that went into propping up the false self can instead be used for life, creativity and love.

Remember that this also requires mental alertness. We are wired by trauma to automatically offer the pleasing and reassuring word. There is nothing wrong with kindness and generosity, but when it is an unconscious impulse, it drains the charge for being alive. Being a nice guy can be a genuine, authentic gesture, or it can be little more than the expression of a two-year-old who has learned the consequences of displeasing. If it's the former, it amplifies the life force. If the latter, it drains the battery. This is an ongoing, daily practice.

The following poem came from a dream I had while writing this chapter.

Theatre of Survival
I dreamt
a psychologist
sat in his cubicle,
doing hair and makeup
for actors in a film.

There is only one profession
for those who
have fallen under the dark,
hypnotic spell
of loved ones
who destroy true beauty
and then cover it up,
whispering that we must not see
or name,
obscuring the wild and tender beauty
that wants to fashion from
our deep yearnings
the one, true story

that is ours alone to live.

In our offices
of unconscious compromise,
we are cosmeticians all,
hair and makeup specialists
in the Theatre of Survival.
Psychologists adjust
Clergy demythologize
Scientists dissect
Pharmacists dispense
Accountants order
Teachers obscure
Engineers encroach
Doctors objectify
Academics parse
Undertakers embalm.

Eros finds no resting place
in this collective cover-up
of the true, whole beauty
which returns painfully
to those unwilling
to keep silent.

The wrinkled, unpainted
face of the hero,
who plays no part
in this drama of deceit,
shines more brightly than the sun.
Planets orbit him,
the lovesick
are drawn to his naked radiance.
The cowardly despise him.
In his light,
the face of cosmetic culture

cakes, salt-stained
by grief.

The learned doctor of religion
comes to the Nazarene peasant,
under cover of night
when the cosmeticians of convention sleep,
asking if a man can be born again,
and of course,
the answer is:
You must.

This unauthorized teacher is no reed
blowing in the wind
fouled by that sad and desperate
survivor's question,
"How might I please you?"
He wipes the face of Nicodemus clean
by the warming fire,
revealing his features
before the alien script arrived
with the invitation to audition.

The angels saw this one
and sang his song to Mary,
who had ears to hear,
and shared his magnificent soul-song
with her friend,
whose own womb leapt with knowing.
This is the expected one,
the welcomed one,
and so his unadorned beauty
redeems the sad and marred
and unwelcomed world
of lost souls.

May your second birth,
dear one,
be likewise into a community
that is expecting you,
a village that has prepared a soft throne
for your incarnation,
that has listened for your soul-song,
and will sing it back to you,
when your slow and blinking eyes
behold the astonishing
mystery anew
and you finally receive
the confirmation you had every right to expect
after the long
and arduous journey
to become human.
Rest now,
on the warm body of
what is truly alive
in the immeasurable beauty
that is you.

CHAPTER 5

The Path of Purification

What is to give light must endure burning.

— **Victor Frankl**

The Purge as Offering

I am puking into my yogurt container, resisting every step of the way. I don't want this, but it's happening and I'm powerless to stop it. I remember somebody mentioned something about "the purge," but this is epic. By the time I'm finished, I am spent, at the edge of my own resources. I pray: "I surrender." It's the equivalent of Jesus's prayer: "Not my will but thine."

My false self is giving way.

I'm frightened.

Then comes the teaching: I am in control of nothing, not when I puke or when I stop puking. The shaman comes and sits in front of me and sings. I puke. When he thinks I'm finished, I'm finished. This is humbling.

The medicine speaks from within: *If you intend to be in relationship with me, I will remove everything that is not love from your body, psyche and spirit. Don't think of this as puking. This is an offering. It's the only offering that I'm interested in. What is coming out of your system is not food. Do you see any food? What is coming out is energetic blocks, memories, trauma, attitudes that are not serving you, hatred that you've stored, entities that found a way in that don't belong, and your false self. I take this offering and metabolize it. I transform the negative energy into energy for life. This is purging, not puking. You are being cleaned from the inside.*

By the time this bout is over, I realize that what I'm being purged of is my self. I mean, the self I *thought* was "me." Every time I see how I made decisions and acted from the false self, I dive for my yogurt container. It is hard to describe how sickening it is to wake up. I described the reason for this in the last chapter: My life was not my own. I hurt people because of this. I lived in deep ignorance but truly believed I was living authentically.

Mortification

Purification can be misconstrued as a process by which we are merely freshening up a self that is in need of a little spring cleaning but otherwise in good shape. However, what I'm talking about here is more radical than this. The separate self of ordinary consciousness needs to die, so absolute is its own falseness, along with the world it sees and the meaning it creates.

Medieval Christians called this process of dying to illusory and incomplete selves "mortification," although the practice came to be associated with all kinds of extreme, masochistic practices, like self-flagellation. Properly understood, "mortification" is a legitimate alternative name for purification. *Mortificatio* is Latin for "putting to death."

I made a partial list of everything in "me" that needed to die. By the time I got to the end of my list, I sincerely wondered if there was anything left of "me."

Mortify:

- my tongue of all malicious and unnecessary talk
- my mind of all opinions, idle speculation and ceaseless talk
- my obsessive worrying about the future and ruminating about the past
- my need to know
- my need to be right
- my sense of entitlement, along with my belief that life should be fair
- my need to make everything about me

- my pessimism, cynicism, judgment of others
- my desire to be in two or more places at once and to do two or more things at the same time
- my belief that I work for money
- my allegiance to the myth of insufficiency
- my fear of having and being nothing
- my need to be liked, to impress, to be smart and clever
- my refusal to accept reality
- my need to create dramas about how I've been wronged

And I was just getting started! What was left of me?

Which makes my point as clearly as anything else. There was nothing left of *that* me. But I felt that there was indeed something or someone left at the end of the process. "I" was left at the end of all these mortifications. What had died wasn't actually "me" at all. What was left was my Heart Self or what Husserl called the "transcendent ego."

I received a mantra to recite during this ceremony: "I am in my heart." What this meant was my "I," my true self, was located in my heart. This "I" hadn't gone anywhere. It was radiant, loving, joyful, equanimous, compassionate, still and creative underneath all the other layers of "me." Atman was still there. The Christ was still there. My Buddha nature was still there. The self that participates in seizing and creating reality was still present. But I had been using an old operating system.

When I purge, I am ridding myself of everything that is in the way of my Heart Self. I'm grateful that early in my journey with ayahuasca I learned to welcome the purge. Every time I purge I end with the question to ayahuasca "Is there anything more? Please take it from me."

A Recipe for Disaster

Let me be clear that we are not born into the world impure. We are born as radiant and unique manifestations of the Great Mystery. Trauma, enacted by those who fail their responsibility for loving us, dims the light we bring with us. Purification is not a matter of overcoming original sin or innate depravity. It's the removal of all that got in the way of our natural light shining brightly because of trauma.

William Law was a heretical Anglican priest and mystic in the 1700s. He said that turning to God without turning from self creates fanatics. The self he advocates turning from is this traumatized self that is concealing our light. When we turn to God without turning from this traumatized self, the implicit self-hatred, and hatred of others, goes underground. But it comes out as "my way or the highway. My truth is the only truth and if you don't believe it you'll end up in hell or you'll be burned to death." Law called this condition "sclerosis of the heart," a hardened heart. If we turn to God without authentic purification, we will spiritualize a false self — and acquire what I call a spiritual ego (see Chapter 16).

Blessed Are the Pure of Heart

In the Beatitudes Jesus says: "Blessed are the pure of heart, for they shall see God." For him, seeing God (spiritual vision) was the end game. Purification, as we've seen, is a turning from the false self — in religious language, the self that is cut off from Source — so that our true nature may take the lead.

At other times Jesus talked about entering the Kingdom of God, which is essentially the same thing as seeing God. There are times on the medicine when you are resting in the Kingdom of God. You feel deep peace — the "peace that passes all understanding." Despite all the trauma and violence that is being worked through in the room, you feel that there is an undeniable perfection about it all. Everything is unfolding as it should.

This intuition of perfection doesn't make rational sense in a world that is morally bankrupt, and if you pop out of this state of consciousness and start thinking too much, you will find a thousand arguments in support of the absurdity of the perception. But somehow, in this condition of pure-heartedness, you trust that all the chaos, violence, hatred, malice, envy, catastrophes, stupidity and ignorance are part of a bigger picture.

Using Jesus's metaphor, the Kingdom of God, or the realm of the divine, includes and enfolds all the bad stuff. Love is the all-encompassing context for evil, hatred, and violence. This is revealed on the medicine. It's not a dogmatic belief. You feel certain that Rhineland mystic Julian of Norwich got it right when she wrote: "All shall be well, and all manner of things shall be well."

These mountaintop experiences, when I connect with the Heart Self and rest in Source, have been an incredible blessing. They came early and powerfully in my ayahuasca journeys. When these bliss moments come, they are like glimpses into an alternate reality — you feel as though you "see God." These glimpses are critically important. When I'm tempted to fall into despair and conclude that the world is a bleak and dreary affair, these "peak experiences" remind me that reality is glorious and life is an inestimable gift.

The goal is to integrate these peak experiences so deeply into our lives that we begin to distrust the absolute claims that the state of despair can make on our lives. This maturation of the soul requires the path of purification. If the pure of heart see God, impurity is obviously an impediment. And if you stay on the path of ayahuasca for any length of time, you will end up consciously purifying the body (what you put in and don't put in); the psyche (your attitudes and beliefs that shape what kind of world you see and your interpretation of experience); and your spirit (your level of dedication, intention and focus).

Purging Trauma

In one of my early journeys I had a vision of indigenous men in a camp inviting me to join them. A huge owl wing covered me, then drew me into the camp of these warriors. They wanted to initiate me into the Order of the Pure Heart. What I didn't realize was how rigorous initiation would be. I thought it was all going to happen in one ceremony. Nice try! Three years later, I feel as though I'm still being prepared for initiation, which will be followed by a lifelong practice of centering in the Heart Self.

In an early ayahuasca ceremony, "nothing" was happening. For two hours the medicine did not come on. No visions, no insights, nada. I tried at first to be patient. But then I became angry and demanding. "Fuck, this is not what I showed up for!"

That's when I realized I was recapitulating what had happened in my early years. The medicine is uber-intelligent.

Confronted as a child with a withholding mother, I grew angry and enraged. At first I protested. I demanded love in the only way I knew how. I took my plate of food in my high chair, defiantly stared down my mother, then turned my plate upside down to dump my food on the floor. The statement I was making was obvious: Food and shelter are not substitutes for love, tenderness and kindness. I won't play along with that game. It's not what I showed up for. I want connection and relationship.

When that protest proved futile, the long process of adapting myself to the conditions of lovelessness ensued.

The medicine was helping me to remember love being withheld. When I got the message, the medicine came on powerfully. I had a vision of a great serpent with feathers slowly passing over me and through my whole system. And then I released sadness. I saw what happened in my early years. More purging.

I learned from this never to believe that "nothing is happening" in a ceremony. What is happening is always the exact thing that needs to happen, even if it feels at first like nothing. I was being purified of the belief that I was the problem.

I have purged attitudes I was unconsciously holding, such as pessimism, cynicism and judgment of others. One time I was in pure bliss and then, out of nowhere, dark clouds rolled in. I got paranoid. Dark entities floated around me, seeking an entry into my body. Outside a ceremony, this would constitute a bad trip. But I asked the medicine why this was happening. She showed me a thought that I had just before the darkness descended. I had held the person beside me in judgment and interpreted his behavior negatively. After I traced the darkness to its origin, in a thought, the darkness lifted. I learned to be mindful about my thoughts, attitudes and beliefs. Thoughts are not inert detritus. They are living beings with the power to bring forth a world that corresponds to them, for good or ill.

I have purged the energetic presence of other people who were feeding off my energy. I have purged particular kinds of food that I had not realized were not good for me (even though these foods were not at the moment in my system). I have purged hatred that belonged to someone else but which I picked up and carried. I have purged broken promises — promises that I made and did not keep. I have purged the hurt I caused others. I have purged ancestral trauma that had nothing to do with me. All of this purging was part of my purification process, and it continues to this day.

My Temptation

In the Jewish tradition, the prophet Malachi foretells of one coming who is "like a refiner's fire, and like fullers' soap" (Malachi 3:2). This one would both cleanse and burn away all that was not holy and righteous. Christians picked up on this prophecy, and Jesus became the fulfillment of it. To follow him was to undergo a baptism by water and by fire.

The purifying and cleansing fire comes, in part, through the ordeal of temptation, something I experienced when I spent seven days alone on the side of a mountain. I was undergoing a weeklong isolation diet. This meant no contact with other people and no food for four days, with a little broth and gruel on the fifth and sixth days. The diet opens and closes with drinking ayahuasca. But the ayahuasca in this setting supports a master plant.

My master plant was Uchu Sanango, an Amazonian tree. I drank this plant every day for four days and prayed to the spirit of the plant for guidance. Then I was to follow my dreams.

The shaman warned us that we would be tested in our dreams, so we had to be alert — even in the dream state!

I received three dreams that were temptation dreams. In the first, my daughter came to me and showed me a spread of the world's finest pastries, all laid out before me. After I cleaned up my drool, I told her that I was on an isolation diet, and this was a test. By satisfying my baser instinct, I would sabotage my higher calling. First test, passed!

In the second dream, pop singer Gwen Stefani appeared, behaving provocatively and wearing, ahem, not much. She was trying to seduce me. I saw what was happening, approached her and tenderly redirected her energies toward her partner, country singer Blake Shelton. I told her that this energy belonged to him, not me.

Finally, in the third dream, I was shopping with my brother. He picked up and, I assumed, purchased a costly pair of binoculars. As I was leaving, I noticed that he had accidentally left them in the store. I took them and handed them to him outside the store. He told me that he hadn't bought them, but what a bonus! Nobody had seen me take the binoculars. They were mine! I was lucid dreaming and knew this too was a test. I returned them.

Binoculars are an interesting symbol. They magnify and clarify vision. The purity of my heart was being strongly tested in dreams involving my baser appetites, my sexuality and my honesty.

Jesus's Temptation

New Testament scholar Walter Wink writes that temptation is always in the direction of the "regressive alternative."[10] Temptations are the distractions that keep us from realizing our evolutionary path and destiny. They try to draw our attention to an easier path, where we remain in the trance of conventional culture. But we must face and know them if we are to transcend them.

The gospels of Matthew, Mark and Luke describe a time when Jesus was tempted to leave the more difficult path. Few take this story seriously, but I do. It shows that Jesus was human, not superhuman, and was not above succumbing to temptation. Therefore, it also shows that Jesus was *actually* contending with his ego. He had to work at it like the rest of us. The ego that believes it is separate and alone in an uncaring universe can only think of taking care of number one and organizing its energies to survive in a hostile world. It cannot trust that the universe "has its back."

This story tells of the Spirit *driving* Jesus into the wilderness after his baptism to get this sorted out. It's not an invitation that Jesus can accept or reject. It is a test that he must go through if he is to fulfill his chosen path. In the story "the Satan" tempts Jesus. The Satan was originally a divine agent, charged with testing the hearts of the righteous. He appears in the story of Job in the Hebrew scripture. By all accounts, Job was a righteous man. But Satan goes to God and says, "Sure, he's righteous now. Everything is coming up roses for him. But take away his prosperity, his property, his family and his health. Then you'll see his true colours." The test is to determine if Job is inner directed or if his character is determined by the winds of circumstance. (Spoiler: Job passes the test.)

The temptation story in the New Testament shows that Jesus was vulnerable, like all human beings, to giving way under pressure. Jesus was on a "diet" according to the story. He was not eating. With the first temptation, Satan tells Jesus to use his extraordinary powers to turn the stones around them into bread and chow down. Jesus responds: "Man shall not live by bread alone but by every word that proceeds from the mouth of God."

---

10 Walter Wink, *Unmasking the Powers: The Invisible Forces That Determine Human Existence* (Minneapolis, MN: Fortress Press, 1986), 21.

We can go through life gorging on the material world, or we can be spiritually nourished by divine guidance. Often that guidance can only be heard when we've deprived ourselves of all the other voices that vie for allegiance, including the gastrointestinal voice! In almost every indigenous and religious tradition, depriving the senses for a time (in order to transcend but include them) is a key element for opening the initiate to the higher spiritual drives. Prematurely indulging basic survival needs short-circuits the higher spiritual aspiration.

After the first temptation fails, Satan tempts Jesus to throw himself off the highest pinnacle of the Temple. Didn't the psalmist say that the angels would come and bear up the righteous? If Jesus truly were the Son of God, surely the angels would save him. The genius of this temptation is that it calls into question both Jesus's mission — *if* you are the Son of God — and his trust in God's goodness, and even his existence. Jesus responds that we are not to put God to the test. Rather, it is *we* who are to be tested. The temptation to believe that we are special, and therefore deserving extraordinary attention, is very strong. It's the flip side, the compensation, for believing that we are worthless.

Finally, Satan claims that it is within his authority to grant Jesus all the kingdoms of the world. He offers them to him. All he requires is that Jesus bow down and worship him. Goethe's play *Faust* builds on this theme of offering our soul's primary allegiance to that which is not God — power, wealth, status and an easy time of life. Jesus counters with the first commandment: "You shall worship God only."

These tests confirm that Jesus's heart is pure. He is ready, willing and able to proceed.

Your Church Is Too Easy

Liberal Christianity soft-sells this demanding aspect of following Christ. The assumption is that everyone present is basically a good person with good intentions, gathering to do a little good in the world and have the occasional potluck dinner. Mark Twain once referred to a man who was "good in the worst sense of the word," which I interpret to mean someone who believes that religion is primarily about being "good." More often than not this kind of person presents a false self. I can be well-behaved, socially appropriate and concerned about all the right things yet lack direct contact with myself or with Source.

Where there is no intentional process of purification, religion becomes little more than a social club. You can't substitute a weekly prayer of confession for all this work.

I recall a story told by Barbara Brown Taylor, an Anglican bishop. Her husband was less interested in the church than in the local First Nation ceremonies. One summer he attended a Sun Dance, a very demanding ceremony. Warriors fast and dance for four days without food in the blazing sun. A fire is kept burning throughout the ceremony, and everybody in attendance holds the dancers in prayer.

On the final day, some dancers may choose to have their chests pierced with a knife, after which a piece of wood is inserted through the incisions. A rope is then attached to the piece of wood and runs from the dancer to a central tree, which signifies the Great Spirit. The dance continues, the dancers who have chosen to be pierced pulling against the tree, signifying that the life of the lower instincts and desires is in service to the Great Spirit. Visions are sought. The ceremony is all about purification, dedication and receiving visions.

When the ceremony ended, a communal dinner was held. With her casserole in hand, Rev. Brown Taylor saw a man in the distance, walking toward her. He looked ragged and somewhat emaciated, but his eyes were on fire and clear. It was her husband. His first words to her were "Your church is too easy."

Buddha's Temptation

I wasn't aware until I was writing this book that the Buddha underwent his own temptations by the devil, who showed up first as Kama, God of Desire, parading three voluptuous women before him.

Unable to distract the Buddha from his concentration, the devil then became Mara, Lord of Death. Hurricanes, torrential rains and showers of flaming rocks bombarded Gautama, but because he had so emptied himself (poverty's true meaning) of his finite self, the weapons found no target to strike and turned into petals as they entered his field of concentration.

Then Mara challenged his right to be doing what he was doing. He was playing on the aspirant's self-doubt. Gautama touched the earth with his right fingertip, and the earth responded, "I bear you witness" with a hundred, a thousand and a hundred thousand roars, whereupon the gods of heaven descended to rapturously tend to the victor.

In one last attempt to deter Gautama from his path, the Lord of Death appealed to reason. How could the average person be expected to understand what the Buddha had discovered? How would he ever translate his wisdom into words? Why bother? Why not just bliss out?

The Buddha answered simply, "A few will understand."

CHAPTER 6

A Man of Sorrow

> *He was despised and rejected by men, a man of sorrows and*
> *acquainted with grief; and as one from whom men hide their*
> *faces he was despised, and we esteemed him not.*
>
> — **Isaiah 53:3**

Purification removes all that is getting in the way of love and opens us up to soul and spirit. As the husk of this self that was forged in trauma and then supported by soulless institutions is shed, we feel the cost of this alienation. Grief rises up and becomes itself a critical expression of purification.

When Bad Trips Are Good

I'm lying in an empty bathtub, six hours into an LSD journey. I spent the first four hours with my therapist. I'm feeling something I've never felt before, and at first I'm not sure what it is. My wife is supporting me. She holds me and rubs my back, but nothing is helping. I'm in the bathtub because I can't get comfortable anywhere else — I've tried every location in the house. I suspect that my mind has led me to the empty bathtub because it reminds me of cold comfort. It's amplifying the feeling I need to get at.

We usually associate being comfortable with our favourite chair, or stretching out on the sofa with a warm blanket. But right now I'm thinking that it refers to our capacity to be comforted — comfort-able, as in able to receive comfort. Which is exactly, in this moment, what I'm not capable of.

I'm regressed. This is a memory. I need comforting but I can find none. I say to my wife, "I think this is sorrow." It's completely new to me. This is what I've been avoiding feeling all my life. It feels like grief on steroids, infinite in depth. It is the feeling of absolute abandonment for which there is no remedy, no end and no escape.

My hunch is that this would constitute what most recreational users of LSD call a "bad trip." It just ain't fun. In the wrong setting it could spin out of control. But the medicine doesn't cause so-called bad trips. The LSD reveals what is already there, in the form of buried memories and experiences.

Forsaken

Psalm 22 comes to mind — as it did for the editors of the gospels trying to understand the crucifixion. When they searched around in their own scriptures for how to describe what Jesus went through, they landed on this heartbreaking lament.

"My God, my God, why have you forsaken me?"

Along with this cry, they lifted the bits about the nails piercing his hands and feet, and the soldiers casting lots for Jesus's clothes. If ever there was a portrait of a man of sorrows, this is it. The poor sod is crying out to God, but it's an echo chamber. Nobody is coming to rescue him. It's pathetic.

In a ceremony in Mexico, the sorrow came up again. I witnessed myself hoping against hope that somebody would come and rescue me. I thought that every person who walked by was coming for me. In my regressed state — I was two years old — I actually thought that they might come to pick me up. But nobody did. They just walked right on by, impervious to my suffering. It was a perfect reenactment of what I went through as a little guy.

"I cry out by day, but you do not answer, and by night, but I find no rest."

The psalmist goes on to lament: 1. It's not fair. 2. You broke my trust. 3. You are all-powerful and I am but a worm of a human being. 4. I am being threatened from every direction and afflicted by terrible diseases. 6.

Still, you are worthy of my undying devotion. 7. You will make it better. I just know it.

I'm paraphrasing. But check it out. It sounds to my ears like a man deprived of maternal affection. Yet he continues to hope against hope that she will come and make it better.

In my regressed state, back at the bathtub, I hear myself say to my wife "She really hurt me. She broke my heart." I am speaking on behalf of a toddler who long ago had to suffer in silence with a deep knowing that he was not loved.

"He was despised and rejected…"

No, my mother doesn't despise me or reject me today. But what I know in my bones is that for the first few years of my life I felt abandoned. I can't say what was going on for her. And what matters in the end is that I not confuse the past with the present.

Motherless

I remember seeing the truth of this last point clearly in an early ayahuasca journey (one I described in Chapter 3). I was trying to rationalize my mother's behavior, defend her and understand both her failure to be tender and her physical violence toward me. That's when I saw on the screen of my consciousness a corrective: FAILURE TO LOVE.

The message was basically: *Stop it! Face reality. Until you do, you will not know yourself. You will never see why your whole life's search for meaning was fueled by an unconscious incredulity about what happened in these formative years. You will not see how your unhealthy patterns of intimacy as an adult replicate your anxious attachment with your mother. You will not understand your irrational rage or how easily shame overtakes you. You will not be able to see this is why you refused for so many decades to ask for what you needed and wanted. You will not be able to understand why your greatest source of shame is your inability to love.*

And then, the kicker.

You couldn't love her. You weren't given the chance. Face it.

But what child doesn't love his mother? Then comes the guilt and the shame I felt as a child, followed by memories of intimate relationships with women that began in love and then fizzled into an inability to sustain. I recall being puzzled because my deepest shame was always my inability to maintain a loving connection. Now it's making sense. I reenacted the conditions of my childhood with women. Clarity arrives. But I feel sick.

Later, in a series of nine ayahuasca journeys in a Mexican jungle, this message is reinforced as I suffer through the longest nights of my life, coming to terms with sorrow and all the feelings I buried as a child. This culminates in my crawling around on my knees, in agony, telling an assistant that I am a "motherless child." The sorrow is unbearable, yet I am being asked to look at it and feel it.

I am sure that this required nine ceremonies because my denial was so deep. I needed to see, in no uncertain terms, that this was part of my story. But I got stuck in the belief that it was my whole story. It was defining me.

The medicine taught me that, no, I am not these feelings. They are memories. Healing began the moment I realized that, as an adult, I have these feelings, but they don't have me. The irony is that the only way to actually accept the feelings is first to be overwhelmed by them — and then to understand that they resurface as memories. They are the past being played out in the present. Until I got real and allowed these feelings to surface, I was powerless to change. I walked around believing that the reality of my childhood was still my reality.

For example, in my state of denial I defaulted to feelings of inadequacy when criticized. I felt shamed by innocuous events and gestures. I could be moody for weeks at a time, walking around with a big Fuck You just under the surface, ready to erupt if anybody disappointed me or crossed me. Mostly, I lived my life under a cloud of unconscious sorrow. My heart had been broken, but until my work with the medicines I didn't know it.

Wasters of Sorrow

The poet Rainer Maria Rilke was a man of sorrow. But he refused to be defeated by it. He glimpsed another possibility: He could assimilate his sorrow in the service of his evolution to a condition that transcended the current order of humanity. This higher order of humans he called "Angels."

> *Some day, emerging at last from this terrifying vision*
> *may I burst into jubilant praise to assenting Angels!*
> *May not even one of the clear-struck keys of the heart*

fail to respond through alighting on slack
or doubtful or rending strings.
May a new-found splendor appear in my streaming face!
My conspicuous Weeping flower!
How dear will you be to me then, you Nights of Affliction!
Oh, why did I not, inconsolable sisters,
more bendingly kneel to receive you,
more loosely surrender myself to your loosened hair?
We wasters of sorrows!
How we stare away into sad endurance beyond them,
trying to foresee their end!
Whereas they are nothing else than our winter foliage,
our somber evergreen,
one of the seasons of our interior year... [11]

By embracing sorrow we make it just "one of the seasons of our interior year." When the medicine brought my sorrow to consciousness, I developed a relationship with that emotion. Relationship implies distance and perspective. I was no longer identified with it.

I then received a new Mother.

Outside the maloca, I made my way to the edge of the jungle. I felt Mother Earth beneath my feet. I looked up and saw the vines and the trees. I turned to my original Mother and saw that she had my back and my feet. She gave me life. She supports me. She gives unceasingly so that life might thrive. I knew that I would never be motherless so long as I could remember that I was being nourished, held and loved by the Great Mother.

When I went back to the maloca, the canopy of trees over us had become a palace of stained glass, studded with fine jewels. The vision was there whether I opened my eyes or closed them. This was the Temple of Mother Ayahuasca, the Great Mother. The sacred feminine surrounded me, supported me, fed and nurtured me. I was not alone, except in memory. I was no longer motherless.

---

11 Rainer Maria Rilke, "Tenth Elegy," in *Duino Elegies*, tr. J.B. Leishman and Stephen Spender.

CHAPTER 7

The Politics of Family

*In effect, they hate us in practice and love us in theory and
induce us to believe them when they define hate as love. The
consequent mystification, confusion and conflict continue to
devastate marriages, families, and each generation of children.*

— **R. D. Laing**

The Dark Side of Family

There's an elephant in the room and it is time to stop talking around it.
I'm not a historian or anthropologist, but my sense is that the moment
humans shifted from village life to the nuclear family, trouble started. Elder
Malidoma Somé writes about village life in Burkino Faso. Still today, every
child has multiple mothers and fathers. The boundaries between families
are more porous. Everything is on public display. In the age of the nuclear
family, generational trauma and the violence of parents against their
children are hidden from public view. If somebody wanted to create an institution in which emotional, physical and sexual abuse could thrive, the
family as we know it in the West would fit the bill.

Trauma expert Bessel van der Kolk opens his book *The Body Keeps Score:
Mind, Brain and Body in the Transformation of Trauma* with some sobering

statistics: "One in five Americans was sexually molested as a child; one in four was beaten by a parent to the point of a mark being left on their body; and one in three couples engages in physical violence. A quarter of us grew up with alcoholic relatives, and one out of eight witnessed their mother being beaten or hit."[12]

These numbers almost certainly underestimate the reality. They do not take into account the emotional trauma of neglect nor of mothers who cannot love their children. As well, early childhood sexual abuse is almost always repressed to the point of total forgetting.

This was a difficult chapter to write. My mother and father are still alive. I have five brothers and sisters. Not one of them wants to read what I'm about to share. I don't know if any of them will, but they were all in the back of my mind as I wrote. I have no desire to cause suffering. In an ideal world, sharing one's own experience shouldn't cause suffering, just curiosity and empathy. But this isn't an ideal world. My narrative of early trauma has not been well received. My father, a very kind and gentle man, threatened that I was on the verge of losing my family. Upon reading in one of my blogs that all was not well in paradise, my mother did not conceal her hurt and rage. This, in turn, set off a flurry of unsympathetic reactions from my siblings.

The prospect of losing my family terrified me at first. I was on the verge of panic for weeks. With some reflection I understood why. In the nuclear family, our parents and siblings are literally our world when we are growing up. In our very early years we are unconsciously terrified of losing them, sure we would not survive if, for whatever reason, they disappeared and we were on our own. In the shock of my family's reaction to me sharing my story of emotional neglect and physical abuse publicly, that ancient terror overtook me. When I understood this, I settled down. Today I am less attached. "Family" has become an abstract concept to me. It is an ideal that no longer exists, except as a sociological category. I don't have a relationship with "family." I have relationships with individuals who are re-

---

12 Quoting V. Felitti et al., "Relationship of Childhood Abuse and Household Dysfunction to Many of the Leading Causes of Death in Adults: The Adverse Childhood Experiences (ACES) Study," *American Journal of Preventative Medicine*, 14, no. 4 (1998): 245–58.

spectful and take my experience seriously — otherwise I am not interested in the relationship.

In writing this chapter, I'm taking my cues from writer and memoirist Anne Lamott, who wrote: "You own everything that happened to you. Tell your stories. If people wanted you to write warmly about them, they should have behaved better."[13] I don't interpret this as a license to rant. I have no need. On the other hand, my family's reaction is textbook.

In his classic study "The Child Sexual Abuse Accommodation Syndrome," Roland Summit describes the secondary trauma associated with the discovery of trauma.[14] When children or, indeed, adults attempt in any way to disclose their experience, they are often met with disbelief, suspicion, threat and denial. This has the effect of reenacting the earlier experience of not being heard, seen or valued — and this explains my panic reaction.

The Evolution of Family in TV and Film

The family is the subject of *Family Guy*, an animated, parodic TV series. The theme song presents the show's subjects, the Griffins family, as the antidote to the loss of "family values" in society. If you've watched the series at all, you see the irony at once. As Reilly Judd Ryan points out in his master's thesis, this same family that sees itself as epitomizing good old family values sells their daughter to pay off pharmaceutical bills; the father nearly marries his own son to collect on a large inheritance; and a diabolical baby schemes to murder his own mother.[15]

There's a reason the show is so popular. Like its predecessor *The Simpsons*, the family dysfunction causes us to guffaw in recognition. It shines a light on the unspoken underbelly of family life. It strikes a chord. Somebody is daring to portray the whole truth and it's a relief to see it exposed. Everybody knows that the family isn't as rosy an institution as it's made

---

13 Anne Lamott, *Bird by Bird: Some Instructions On Writing and Life* (New York: Anchor Books, 1995).

14 Roland C. Summit, "The Child Sexual Abuse Accommodation Syndrome," *Child Abuse and Neglect* 7 (1983): 177–93.

15 Reilly Judd Ryan, "Where Are Those Good Old-Fashioned Values? Family and Satire in *Family Guy*" (master's thesis, Brigham Young University, 2015), https://scholarsarchive.byu.edu/etd/5583/.

out to be. Hollywood has produced a plethora of films devoted to the family getting together for the holidays with disastrous results, and Netflix has a whole genre called "The Dysfunctional Family." The truth underlying the image is exposed and it is devastating.

The Danish film *The Celebration* comes to mind. It's no satire, however. The family gets together to celebrate the sixtieth birthday of the family patriarch. He is apparently highly respected. But all is not well. His daughter has just committed suicide and the whole family is in denial. The father asks the eldest son to say a few words during the dinner. The son has prepared two speeches, one written on green paper and the other on yellow. He asks his father to choose which one he should deliver. The father chooses the green one, which the son announces is the "speech of truth." The father becomes nervous. The son reveals the truth of why his sister took her own life: the father raped both the son and his sister. The family is thrown into disarray.

This kind of truth telling is the exception still today. The family continues to be a fiercely defended institution, from within and without. Until *The Simpsons* and *The Family Guy,* television reflected a romantic and saccharine image of the family, as Brent Mills shows in his examination of the evolution of the TV family sitcom.[16] I grew up watching *Leave It to Beaver* reruns, a TV series depicting the Andersons as the perfect, intact, nuclear family. This show and *The Adventures of Ozzie and Harriet* give examples of what Mills calls the "stable family unit." Next came the "surreal" family system with *The Munsters, The Adams Family* and *Bewitched* in the 1960s. Right in your own neighbourhood, these series suggest, lives a family that does not fit the mold. Still, these families, while strange, are benign. The Reaganite era saw the advent of the "secure" families — *Family Ties* and *The Cosby Show* — along with the surrogate workplace families of *Cheers* and *Taxi*. None of these genres contend with the gritty truth. That the star of *The Cosby Show* was recently convicted of aggravated indecent assault is not lost on me. Dozens of women came forward with accusations that he first drugged and then raped them.

---

16   Brent Mills, *The Sitcom*, TV Genres (Edinburgh: Edinburgh University Press, 2009).

Family Guy exposes the myth that "the family" as an unambiguous good is an illusion. What we call family is sets and subsets of relationships, which may or may not be "good," depending on how much love, tenderness and kindness is present, along with how much conscious intention there is to encourage the maturation of unique individuals.

Those who miss the nature and function of parody decry the program's immorality and subversion of family values. Yet parody is precisely the form required to deconstruct the pervasive sentimentalizing of family in our society — a lie that has been perpetrated at least since the Victorian age, but that we will see existed as far back as biblical times and before. *Family Guy*'s gallows humor makes the exposé bearable, slipping the truth in under our defenses.

Parody functions like parable, the form Jesus chose to deliver his bombshells. Myth (not in the sense of a false statement but as an overarching cultural narrative that conveys a worldview) constructs a world. Parable and parody explode that world. They function apocalyptically, announcing the end of a world built on illusion and fantasy.

Shining the light of conscious awareness on the true dynamics of our family system has the same impact as do parody and parable on myth. Every new insight into the truth of our experience acts like a small explosion of awareness that deconstructs the myth of the happy family.

Defending the Perpetrator

Scottish psychiatrist R. D. Laing cautioned against exposing the myth of "good old family values" and taking a cold, hard look at inherited blueprints. (By "blueprints" I mean the rules, norms and worldviews that the institution of the family overlay on children without conscious awareness. We think we are free, but actually we've constructed the architecture of our life based on that blueprint.)

"If anyone in the family begins to realize that he is a shadow of a puppet, he will be wise to exercise the greatest precautions as to whom he imparts this information," Laing wrote. "It is not 'normal' to realize such things. There are a number of psychiatric names, and a variety of treatments, for such realizations.

"I consider many adults (myself included) are or have been, more or less, in a hypnotic trance, induced in early infancy: we remain in this state until — when we dead awaken, as Ibsen makes one of his characters say — we shall find that we have never lived. Attempts to wake before our time are often punished especially by those who love us most. Because they are, bless them, still asleep."[17]

I've described how my naïve attempts to share my experience met with violent backlash from family members. The intent of this onslaught could be interpreted as an attempt to induce a renewed hypnotic state in me. The purported suffering that I was supposedly causing is a secondary, neurotic form of suffering. It is suffering aroused by a refusal to accept the truth of an individual family member's experience. Accept the truth, feel it, be curious, make amends and the drama is over.

I have seen many clients who, when sharing their own experience of mistreatment, were faced with the same accusation of causing suffering to the parents and the family. As I said earlier, this accusation is a repeat of the original violence. Often the perpetrators claim that the innocent child brought the violence on himself with bad behavior. But my clients were not asking for anything, as children or as adults, except to be known and taken seriously. They were not blaming or shaming.

The refusal to accept the existence of actual suffering (reality) in order to protect the image of the perfect family is an exercise of power — power as domination. When family members isolate and shun another family member who claims that she has been sexually abused, they are unconsciously exercising this power. This has the effect of reenacting the original trauma, a kind of punishment for exposing the myth of the ideal family.

The exercise of this power is political. In *The Politics of the Family*, R. D. Laing exposed how the label "schizophrenia" came to apply to those individuals in a family system whose best solution to the inherent but unconscious violence of parents was to escape into madness. The medical system then developed an elaborate system that initiated the "patient" into madness: hospitalization, a label for the illness, medication and follow-up programs that had the effect of protecting the family from any responsibility

17   R.D. Laing, *The Politics of the Family and Other Essays* (New York: Vintage Books, 1972).

for creating the condition. This amounted to imprisoning the identified patient and could be seen as a protection racket designed to defend the romantic ideal of the family.

In 1860, one of the first psychiatrists, Professor Bénédict Morel of France, described the case of a thirteen-year-old boy, who was sent by his father for treatment. The son, a very intelligent and advanced boy, had developed a violent hatred for his father that had replaced "the most tender sentiments." The boy was promptly sent away to be fixed by the latest psychiatric methods but proved resistant to treatment. He was diagnosed with dementia praecox, what we now call schizophrenia. The son regressed in the treatment, lost all of his intellectual ability and from that point forward was institutionalized. Not once did anyone ask, "Why did the boy hate his father?"[18]

Several decades later, Sigmund Freud played the same role, defending the Victorian ideal of family when confronted with the reports of his (primarily) female patients that their fathers had sexually abused them. At first he believed his patients and presented his findings publicly. But he faced ridicule and the sanction of his professional circle in Vienna. Under pressure, he retracted. Then he developed an elaborate theory of infantile sexual fantasy. Essentially, he concluded that his female patients fabricated the sexual abuse.

From then on, the diagnosis of hysteria became the most popular female diagnosis. The etymology of hysteria is "suffering in the uterus." But, according to Freud, the women's own sexual fantasies caused the uterine suffering, not the unimaginable violence enacted against them by their own fathers. Again, the family image is defended at all costs.

This is still going on in psychoanalytic circles. Toward the end of her life, Alice Miller refused the title of psychoanalyst, so disillusioned was she with her profession. She had undergone two complete cycles of analysis, but neither of her analysts challenged her portrayal of her family as "happy" and "well-adjusted." It was only after doing art therapy that she discovered her own childhood abuse. Why were her analysts not able to see through her denial and repression? Was it because they were taught to regard many

---

18 Ibid., 69.

forms of abuse as "proper upbringing" or "training for their own good"? Perhaps they had never exited the hypnotic trance themselves.

Abused family members are often the rare ones who awaken from the trance. It is a rude and painful awakening. If there is a blessing in the experience of abuse, it consists in this alone. Victims face a choice: either repress all that they know and allow the truth of their experience to die with them, often at the cost of their own health; or speak up, expose the family myth and face shunning, isolation and the extended family's assumption that they are a bad and/or crazy person for choosing to hurt the family so much. The latter choice requires exceptional courage and exceptional support from good friends, family and therapists.

Family as Cult

When a family defends its secrets over the truth of the individual family member's experience, it is a cult, not a family. A cult, any cult, cannot abide members' expressions of individuality, doubt, questioning of core beliefs, challenging of norms and rules, or taking a higher perspective on what is really happening. Finally, a cult will absolutely not allow individuals to trust their own experience as authoritative. As soon as individuals achieve such an awakening, they are already banished. The trance is broken. Awareness is an act of self-banishment. And then, if the backlash of the leadership and membership of the cult do not evoke a renewed obedience, the abused individuals must escape — into madness or by leaving, never to return.

Under stress, families function like a cult. This is why our health care budgets are chronically strained, the rate of addiction in our society is epidemic and the recidivism rates in our prison systems are so high. People must escape the stranglehold of their families, one way or another.

Honour Your Mother and Your Father

One of the laws at the heart of all religion is that you shall honour your mother and father. This is explicit in the fifth of the Ten Commandments of Judaism, but it's there in all the other religions. You do this, according to the commandment, so you might live long and prosper. If you fail to honour them, there are procedures for your father to make a case against you, which could result in a son or daughter being stoned to death.

Don't you find it curious, however, that there would need to be any law imposed when it comes to honouring parents. Lao Tzu, the Chinese philosopher associated with the Tao Te Ching, said that when the *Tao* (the natural way) breaks down, man introduces laws. In the presence of love and respect, we naturally confer that same love and respect on parents. Both are natural and spontaneous conditions, freely offered and exchanged. The need to impose respect through a law backed up by the death penalty conceals a story of family violence.

Historically, the state has counted on families to turn out acquiescent citizens. Families can become the breeding ground for totalitarian regimes, encouraging what French philosopher Michel Foucault called "governmentality." This describes citizens' unconscious internalization of state values so that these values need not be externally imposed by a police force. The family is the tool of the state in eliciting conformity. If children experience inhumane treatment at home, yet emerge with the fantasy that they had a happy childhood, the state can pretty much count on acquiescence to inhumane policies.

An example of this was provided by the National Football League during its 2016 season. When quarterback Colin Kaepernick of the San Francisco 49ers protested police brutality against blacks by sitting or kneeling during the national anthem before football games, he set off a furious backlash. Patriotic white people, upholders of "good old family values," were outraged. How dare he use a sports event to make a political statement? (The irony was profound. What almost everybody lost sight of was the fact that singing the national anthem before a sports event is an inherently political gesture.) Kaepernick had broken an implicit agreement not to speak out against the violence of the state. The owners of the league punished him. No team would pick up his contract. Donald Trump attempted to reframe his actions as a protest against the flag.

The connection between exposing the myth of one big happy family and exposing the myth of America the Great is apparent. Nobody wants to be awakened to the violence of the family or to the state's violence against the innocent. Singing the national anthem before a sports event is the hypnotic induction of allegiance and obedience. Outrage against Kaepernick is the same outrage, on a larger scale, directed against uppity family members who dare to speak out about the reality of their experience.

The Hard Sayings of Jesus

But what about Christianity? Doesn't Christianity unequivocally support the sanctity of family? Jesus was Jewish. The commandment to honour his father and mother was drilled into him. But somehow he had sufficiently separated himself from his religion, his family and the Roman state (which was invested in turning out Roman citizens and not individuals). The so-called hard sayings of Jesus, which have perplexed scholars for hundreds of years, all relate to family.

He was teaching one day when his disciples came up to him and told him that this mother and his siblings were outside. His surprising response was to ask the crowd, "Who are my mother and my brothers?" Then he pointed to his disciples and said, "These are my mother and my brothers. Those who do the will of my Father are my mother and brothers and sisters" (Matthew 12:48).

Jesus started a new family — his disciples — based on a new set of values: those who do the will of the Father. For followers of Jesus, this means eschewing all forms of violence, particularly against children, as we will see. Allegiance to the family based on nothing but blood ties, ideals and religious laws meant nothing to Jesus.

In Mark's gospel there is a story of people bringing children to Jesus to be blessed. His disciples tried to stop them because the children were street children and therefore fatherless. Without the protection of a father, they occupied the lowest rung on the social ladder. They were expendable. By preventing the children's contact with Jesus, the disciples were enacting the cultural norms that labeled these "urchins" invisible and disposable. But Jesus rebuked the disciples, telling them, "To such belong the Kingdom of God." Then he took the children in his arms and blessed them. This was a radical gesture. When a father blessed a child it formalized that he was taking the child into his home. He entered into a covenant of protection. Jesus's blessing of the children is all the more poignant given the possibility that he himself was fatherless. He knew what it felt like to be expendable. (Mark 10:13–16).[19] This story is unequivocal affirmation of Jesus's advocacy for neglected and abused children.

At another time he shocked his followers, and no doubt his detractors, by saying: "If anyone comes to me and does not hate his own father and mother and wife and children and brothers and sisters, yes, and even his own life, he cannot be my disciple" (Luke 14:26).

This is a teaching by a man who privileged individual responsibility over allegiance to a family code. "Hating oneself" is consistent with waking up to the truth that the social self we constructed to meet the needs of the family and state needs to undergo a death. We need to be reborn if we are to become individuals. This death of the constructed or adapted self, as we've seen, is the heart of all authentic spiritual paths.

No, Jesus wasn't a cult leader who advocated blind obedience to himself. Quite the opposite. This saying is an invitation to freedom. To the degree that one's own mother and father were functioning as little more than fashioning tools of the state or the dominant religion, they needed to be left behind. Yes, "hate" is a strong word. But I do find it interesting that in LSD sessions, I found a substrate of hatred formed very early in life. Because it was socially unacceptable as well as in my best (survival) interests I repressed it. If this hatred is contained in childhood — that is, allowed to be expressed — it is released and is harmless. But if there is no space for a toddler to express it, and in fact, if she is punished for expressing these feelings, they will go underground. Then, the hatred is destructive because it is unknown and denied.

But to "hate" consciously is to use this underground river of energy constructively. We can transmute all that energy by refusing to go along with values and behaviors that instilled blind obedience to authority. These systems of domination (the state, religion and family) often instill obedience through fear. Jesus is offering the sharp sword of differentiation, for the purpose of liberation. This wielding is what I believe Jesus meant by "hating", the courage to finally and decisively cut all ties to that which binds us.

---

19 See A.G. Van Aarde, "Jesus' Affection towards Children and Matthew's Tale of Two Kings," *Acta Theologica*, 24, no. 2 (2004): 127–46.

I linger on these hard teachings of Jesus because the evangelical right wing of the church regards "family values" to be the very core of Christian teachings. No politicians in the United States can win election until they solemnly proclaim their allegiance to these values. And it's not only the right wing of the church. Liberal Christians, in my experience, have yet to deconstruct this myth — despite having been exposed to and taken a stand against every other form of systemic injustice imaginable. The left wing of the church remains blind to the violence being perpetrated against children in its own membership.

Again, Jesus says: "Do not think that I came to bring peace on the earth: I did not come to bring peace, but a sword. For I came to set a man against his father and a daughter against her mother, and a daughter-in-law against her mother-in-law, and a man's enemies will be the members of his own household. He who loves father or mother more than me is not worthy of me; and he who loves son or daughter more than me is not worthy of me. And he who does not take up his cross and follow after me is not worthy of me" (Matthew 10:34–37).

It's not much wonder that scholars call these "hard sayings." They undermine the very foundations of a society that is based on conventional "family values." If one has never called into question allegiance to the family as the foundation of society, these teachings are disruptive. More, if one believes that Jesus was all about shoring up conventional family values, these teachings amount to an apocalyptic correction. *You will find not a shred of support for "traditional family values" in the New Testament.*

These traditional values, which most Christians assume Jesus is all about, are in fact the "peace" he is rejecting. Instead he brings a sword, an apt metaphor for differentiation. The sword of higher consciousness pierces through conventional values and beliefs, dividing, rather than uniting, the family. Only those who wield this sword will gain their freedom.

Jesus wasn't trashing his biological family. But he was contradicting the conventional adage that blood is thicker than water. In this he was consistent with his mentor, John the Baptist. When John saw the religious authorities coming to be baptized, he made it abundantly clear that sharing a bloodline with Abraham would not save them from the wrath (violence) to come. Blood ties would not save them because the most effective vehicle for transmission of violence happens through those blood ties. The "wrath that is to come," in John's words, is precisely unredeemed violence, and uncritical allegiance to family guarantees its unconscious transmission (Matthew 3:7–9).

The alternative, for Jesus, was to find a new family — those who do the will of God. The disciples were this new family. To "follow Jesus" meant to follow in his ways, and this meant turning away from all that was violent, repressive and allegiant to that which was not holy. This potentially included one's own family and the empire of Caesar, which sought peace through violence (false unity). To be born again was to enter a family characterized by love — divine love enacted in the human realm is the Kingdom of God.

Jesus's teaching held up individual sovereignty, responsibility and self-expression over loyalty to the collective, including family. In this he anticipated the American and French revolutions nearly eighteen centuries later. The radical implication is a shift from a false unity that sacrifices individuality to a true unity in which the uniqueness of the individual is encouraged and then offered in support of a more robust community.

Buddha and Family

The Buddha beat Jesus to the punch. Over five hundred years before Jesus, Siddhartha Gautama, who came to be known as the Buddha, or the Enlightened One, set the stage for placing the individual and the truth over family and adherence to tradition. He walked away from his royal family and privilege. Legend has it that fortune-tellers told his father that he would be a great man. If he remained with the world, he would become a great king and unify India. But if he renounced the world, he would become a world saviour. His father was invested in Siddhartha remaining attached to the world and went to great lengths to ensure that he never experienced disease, decrepitude or death. (This violated his son's sovereignty, masquerading, no doubt, as loving concern).

Inevitably, his son experienced all three dreaded realities. In the middle of the night, in what is called The Great Going Forth, he left his wife and son, shaved his head, dressed in "ragged raiment" and entered the forest in search of enlightenment. The Buddha's first act of liberation was to escape the tyranny of his family. It was a political act, a move against the family as a political institution established to perpetuate the values of the state. And although he taught about the importance of *Sangha* (community), the focus always remained on individuals achieving enlightenment for themselves. Community supports individual enlightenment but is not an end in itself.

Yet still today, individuating ourselves — that is, becoming an individual and distinguishing ourselves from the collective norms of a larger group, like a family or peer group remains one of the most difficult journeys we can make. This is because there remains an implicit and unconscious commitment to honour our mother and father — we don't want to hurt them by telling the truth of our experience. It is often painful to become an individual. But remember, we have to learn that becoming our unique self hurts others. The power of our impulse to default to false unity at all costs is enormous because it is a memory of a time when we couldn't survive without the family's approval and resourcing.

When I was twenty-nine I had a dream in which I was going home, bringing my fluffy new puppy to show to the family. I had just walked in the door when the family dog, an apparently loving black Lab, jumped up and grabbed my puppy by the throat. He began violently shaking him. Blood was flying all over. I was faced with a choice. Kill the family dog to save my puppy. Or let the family dog kill my puppy. I strangled the beloved family dog and walked away in sadness, knowing they would never accept what I had done.

This is an individuation dream. My little puppy in the dream is my true self that I want to share with the family. The family dog that threatened this new life is the shadow side of families that refuses to allow any new life, especially if that life threatens the core allegiance to family.

Thou Shalt Not Be Aware

Alice Miller formulated an eleventh commandment: "Thou shalt not be aware." She bases it on the story of creation in Genesis. God forbids Eve to eat the fruit from the tree of good and evil. But the snake has it right. The gods or God know that if Eve does eat the fruit, her eyes will be opened — that is, she will become aware of good and evil from within. She will no longer need priests, or laws, to tell her what to think or how to behave. Her awakening threatens the edifice of institutional religion. She becomes an individual.

This commandment to not be aware is enforced, overtly or covertly, by family members. With sexual abuse, enforcement often comes in the form of an explicit warning by the perpetrator to never speak of the violence. But even if it's not explicit, the mechanisms of denial and repression, along with the invalidation of the victim's experience, ensure obedience to this commandment — Thou shalt not be aware.

Mystic, philosopher and spiritual teacher G. I. Gurdjieff believed that the first task of the person seeking spiritual wholeness is to break the spell of hypnosis that we all live under. P. D. Ouspensky, a student and biographer of Gurdjieff, recounts this story:

> There is an Eastern tale that speaks about a very rich magician who had a great many sheep. But at the same time this magician was very mean. He did not want to hire shepherds, nor did he want to erect a fence about the pasture where the sheep were grazing. The sheep consequently often wandered into the forest, fell into ravines and so on, and above all, they ran away, for they knew that the magician wanted their flesh and their skins, and this they did not like.
>
> At last the magician found a remedy. He hypnotized his sheep and suggested to them, first of all, that they were immortal and that no harm was being done to them when they were skinned; that on the contrary, it would be very good for them and even pleasant; secondly he suggested that the magician was a good master who loved his flock so much that he was willing to do anything in the world for them; and in the third place, that if anything at all were going to happen to them, it was not going to happen just then, at any rate not that day, and therefore they had no need to think about it. Further, the magician suggested to his sheep that they were not sheep at all; to some of them he suggested that they were lions, to some that they were eagles, to some that they were men, to others that they were magicians.

After this all his cares and worries about the sheep came to an end. They never ran away again, but quietly awaited the time when the magician would require their flesh and skins.[20]

This story brilliantly captures the human condition. We believe that we are free, but are we? We believe that our parents love us and "would do anything for us," but is it true? We believe our hypnotizers are good people, but how would we know? We believe that no serious harm has been or will be done to us, but are we taking ourselves seriously enough? We believe that there is no reason to even think about it, but who and what are we protecting with this belief? We go on placidly grazing, and we grow up to be the hypnotizers of future generations.

There is a strong compulsion in all of us to return to the Garden of Eden before our inner feminine eats the apple and awakens. We want to remain in our slumber because waking up might cost us our family. We might be shamed and cast out, as Eve was driven from the garden of the idealized family. Being forbidden to eat the fruit of the tree of the knowledge of good and evil is a poetic way of describing the urge to remain unconscious. Our first true awakening is seeing what actually happened to us in our families. It means awakening to the trauma that is at the root of so much suffering.

The ancient Jews understood that families transmitted violence to future generations.

The Lord, a God merciful and gracious, slow to anger and abounding in steadfast love and faithfulness, keeping steadfast love for thousands, forgiving iniquity and transgression and sin, but who will by no means clear the guilty, visiting the iniquity of the fathers on the children, and the children's children, to the third and fourth generation. (Exodus 34:6–7)

Focus on the last line. The children of subsequent generations pick up the tab for the father's "iniquity." Presumably this is what the writer means when he writes that while God is forgiving, "he" will not "clear the guilty." Most men who sexually abuse their daughters believe that what they are doing is not so bad, and besides, she won't remember. But here's a warning

---

20 P. D. Ouspensky, *In Search of the Miraculous* (London: Routledge and Kegan Paul, 1950), 219.

to them: Your evil lives on in your ancestry. You are the cause of misery to the third and fourth generations.

Science is confirming this ancient intuition that trauma is passed down the generational line at least to the third generation. It even alters the DNA. Through no fault of her own, a daughter can inherit the unredeemed trauma of a grandmother or a grandfather. Mark Wolynn summarizes the science in his book *It Didn't Start with You: How Inherited Family Trauma Shapes Who We Are and How to End the Cycle.* He gathered stories of men and women who lived with severe depression, anxiety and sorrow, conditions that resisted every form of treatment. But when these individuals looked at their family histories a few generations deep, they uncovered trauma that was never resolved. Guess who gets to resolve it? Not really fair. But then, as we'll discover in the next chapter, life isn't fair.

So what do we do with this information? The realization that our own parents were themselves likely victims of trauma, as were their parents and so on…all the way back to who knows when it started, is sobering. It leaves us with nobody to blame. We are responsible, as adults, for the quality of our lives. Once we were innocent victims, but as adults we can do the work that enables us to take responsibility for our lives. In ayahuasca ceremonies, you and everybody else in the room purges this generational trauma. The work is not just for your healing. It's for your whole ancestral lineage. Your personal healing is redemptive work — redeeming the violence and other forms of trauma that got passed down to you.

This is a sacred calling. There is no more important work for the future of our species. Parenting is a high and holy calling. We pass either a legacy of love or a legacy of violence on to our children and our children's children. The most effective way to evolve human consciousness is to end violence, starting with ourselves and our children. We can orient toward our children in such a way that they realize they are not our property. They are not ours to do whatever we please with. They belong to the future. We are temporary stewards, and our children are entrusted to us for a short time, on behalf of society, so they may know and live into their truest calling. We need to refuse the societal mandate to "shape" them into good citizens or economic producers. We can learn the subtle art of letting them be while protecting and nurturing them for the short time they are in our care. We can show them that it is possible to never be freer than when they are in relationship, such is the level of safety, trust and acceptance they know in our presence. We can commit to never, under any circumstances, using them for our own pleasure, shaming them or raising a hand to them in anger. We can teach them that it is safe to relax and to trust their own experience as the final arbiter of what is right for them.

The question remains, though: What do you do when the light goes on and you see that family is not all that it is cracked up to be and that you were hurt by those you trusted to care for you? Forgiveness is undoubtedly the most advocated key to healing in the majority of religions and new age spirituality. In the next chapter I sound a cautionary note.

CHAPTER 8

Suffering and Forgiveness

There is a great deal of pain in life and perhaps the only pain that can be avoided is the pain that comes from trying to avoid pain.

— R. D. Laing

The Rush to Forgive

"But you forgive her, right?"

I have just come out of the most grueling of all my ayahuasca ceremonies. I saw what happened to me as a baby and a toddler. I relived the feelings associated with a mother who wasn't available to give me the love, attention and tenderness I needed. I felt the terror of seeing her rage and of being hit. The question caught me off guard. In fact, in the midst of the ceremony, I did feel compassion for her and for myself. But somehow, no, it didn't feel like forgiveness.

We hurt each other. God forgives. That's what religions teach, right? But do we? Should we? Are there conditions? Do we unconditionally forgive? If there are conditions, what are they? We're not God. We're human. What do we do when our hearts are broken?

I've wrestled with forgiveness in my career as a Christian minister. I advocated forgiving others for the reasons we've all heard: it's not about the person who wronged us, it's about our own spiritual well-being and freedom; by holding a grudge we're hurting ourselves and giving our perpetrator power to control us; we're making ourselves sick — hell, we might end up with cancer.

All this may be true, but there's something about the rush to forgive that I distrust. This is particularly true when people who have mistreated us are not asking for forgiveness, or ask forgiveness with no interest in hearing about the impact their actions had on us. They don't want forgiveness; they want to be let off the hook. It's one thing to feel compassion for our perpetrator. But feeling compassion for them is not the same as forgiveness.

In *The Tears of the Ancestors,* Daan van Kampenhout interviews a respected rabbi about the difference between compassion and forgiveness. A prison guard in a Nazi concentration camp had murdered the rabbi's father and countless other Jews. The man responsible, now in his late eighties, was appearing before an international tribunal. The rabbi saw the old man, bent over, shuffling into the courtroom and waving at members of his family as he passed them. The rabbi felt genuine compassion for the former guard, for his sore back, for how he was just being an obedient soldier during the war to feed his family. He felt compassion for the grandchildren seeing their beloved grandpa having to undergo this interrogation. And then the rabbi says: "But still, if they had hung him, and I was asked to push the lever that would make him fall and die, I would do it. I would do it, if they would ask it from me, without hesitation."

This shocks us because we are so accustomed to hearing only dramatic stories of forgiveness. But there is something about the rabbi's perspective that represents an important corrective.

Why is there so much pressure to get so quickly to forgiveness? My hunch is that this is what lies behind those stories of mothers who forgive the murderer of their daughter a week after the crime. Often they are conservative Christians, who would be feeling considerable pressure, from within and without, to forgive. From within, good Christians want to be faithful disciples of Jesus. Didn't he tell us to forgive seven times seventy times? From without, I sense a pastor who perceives it is his role to encourage forgiveness as soon as possible. The cynic in me knows that forgiveness testimonies make the best sermons.

I take these public gestures of forgiveness with a grain of salt. In my own case it took a couple of years before I had uncovered the true impact of my trauma on my life. If I had jumped to forgiveness too quickly, I would have forfeited the opportunity for deep integration — before I even knew the full extent of what I was forgiving. In one ceremony, the wisdom I received told me to suspend the concern for forgiveness for the time being.

In the meantime, the bottom line was "do not hate." To hate is to leave the path of love. Even so, (as we saw in the last chapter) it's okay to allow *feelings* of hatred to emerge and then let them go. Carrying around hate is spiritually enervating. I remember as a little kid being overwhelmed when I was alone in my bedroom, hating my mother for the unfairness of what happened. What was not okay, according to the wisdom that came to me on the medicine, was to act out that hate as an adult.

Flight to Transcendence

The phrase "flight to transcendence" describes the tendency, when dealing with heartbreaking acts of violence against self or others, to leave the body and occupy the mind of God. We jump out of our skin and into the mind and heart of God. It's possible to do this. We can enter so-called non-dual states through meditation and get a view of the situation from sixty thousand feet. From this lofty vantage point, we see the whole history of violence. We understand, for example, that a murderer himself was traumatized as a child, as was his father before him. We see this murderer from the perspective of unity consciousness as a child of God. Who are we not to forgive?

This happened to me in the ayahuasca ceremonies. I saw the abuse of my parents and the abuse of their parents, going back generations. I felt for them, and I felt a general compassion for all humanity. This was a God's-eye view of what happened to me, and it is legitimate.

But as the medicine wore off, I came back into my body and mind. I noticed that here I was a little less quick to embrace forgiveness. We comprise body, psyche and spirit, and each of these domains is sovereign and needs to be honoured — not just the spiritual dimension. Spiritually, when in the medicine, I was in the mind and heart of God. The act was already forgiven. I mean, God is unconditional love, after all, and I was united with God in the medicine.

But my body and my psyche needed to catch up. Once you step out of spirit into soul or psyche, and then again into body, there is work to be done. This takes time. To ignore this work is the very definition of spiritual bypassing.

The temptation to bypass is powerful. We want to be spared the downward spiral of grief, sorrow, rage and hatred we feel in response to such indignity. While this natural tendency to escape what's happened to us is understandable, the only way out is the way through. Without going through it, I would never have known the depth of my sorrow and why people often commented about an energetic sadness they saw in me, even when things were going well. I would never have known why I had so much rage.

In my LSD sessions I tapped into that infinite pool of rage, along with hatred. These simmered below the surface, just waiting for someone to wrong me so that I could let loose. And without awareness of the origin of these feelings, I unconsciously created the conditions in my life that justified my being enraged. I could then point to the conditions I had unconsciously created and argue that my hatred, cynicism and pessimism about the human condition were legitimate.

I've mentioned my isolation retreat on the mountain. Forgiveness was one of the central themes of this retreat. My master plant (Uchu Sanango) is a truth teller. I called upon the spirit of this plant and prayed to him for seven days. I was surprised to be asked to set aside forgiveness and instead learn about suffering.

Here's the teaching I received on the medicine:

1. Life is suffering.
2. It isn't fair.
3. There's no escaping it.

Let's take these one at a time. I quoted R. D. Laing at the beginning of the chapter. He is saying that there is the direct suffering of a wrong committed against us, and then there is the indirect suffering that is caused by denying it. This is neurotic pain that we inflict on ourselves and others. Neurotic pain is the suffering we undergo unconsciously — the destructive patterns of intimacy, the addictions, the "depression," the anxiety. When the root cause is uncovered and we feel what happened, the neurotic pain ends. We stop hurting others the way we've been hurt, and we stop hurting ourselves. Then the clean, healing suffering begins.

A Deeper Meaning of the Passion of Christ

Christians talk about the "passion" of Christ. There's a whole season, Lent, devoted to tracking Jesus's journey into his suffering. It doesn't mean that he was a man of passion, like Zorba the Greek. The word "passion" derives from the Latin *passio,* which means "to suffer." The word "passive" is also derived from this Latin root. The connection is found in what French priest and paleontologist Pierre Teilhard de Chardin called "the passivities." These are the vagaries and vicissitudes of life, the stuff we must passively endure or undergo — illnesses, accidents, violence, natural catastrophes and death. This is the condition of contingency, the realization that things happen in life for which we can never be fully prepared. It's possible to do a metaphysical sleight of hand and make the claim that we choose literally everything in life, including being raped by our father. But this new age posturing always strikes me as a way of maintaining the illusion of control in a world that is clearly not in our control.

This is why the crucifixion is called the passion of Christ. He had to undergo it. When he cries from the cross the words of the Psalmist, "My God, why have you forsaken me," this was a man crying out to God in a world that was beyond his control. It was his passivity to undergo what he did not choose. The author of the gospel of John is unable to accept this, so he presents Jesus as totally in control of his destiny, right up to and including his crucifixion. But then, this gospel is distinct from the others in the way the author presents Jesus as more divine than human.

Teilhard de Chardin estimates that as much as 75 percent of our life is about undergoing the passivities. In effect, we're all involved in our own passion play with Christ. If his estimate is anywhere near accurate, the only form of control we have is how we respond to being out of control. We can be control freaks and try to maintain the illusion of control. Or we can accept that life is suffering and, within that constraint, be as creative as possible in how we respond.

Life Isn't Fair

On the mountain, I was taken to the very edge of insanity. Actually, I was taken to the very edge of reality. It only feels insane because the world I had assumed was real isn't. The self I had constructed to adapt to the world learned to get along with insanity. There's time to think up there, lots of time. Or perhaps it is more accurate to say that there is a lot of time to *be* thought. It feels like I'm entertaining thoughts not produced by me. I used the time to unpack the thought that life should be fair.

When we are violated, our mind forms a thought that our perpetrator owes us. Those who have wronged us, we believe, are in debt to us. This is why vigilante movies, like *Taken* or *Unforgiven,* are so popular. I'm convinced that most of us carry around unconscious violations, and we gain vicarious satisfaction when we see the story of vengeance being played out right before our eyes. Someone is collecting on the debt. Some evil person is getting exactly what he or she deserves — death, preferably in as gruesome a form as possible. Deep down, in our shadow selves, we feel that the appropriate response to being hurt by others is to end their lives.

This is why, in the Lord's Prayer, we ask to have our debts forgiven as we forgive the debts of others. To "forgive debts" means to give up the belief that an individual, and by extension life, owes something to us — a belief that leads to violence in one form or another.

What we don't realize is that even if we collected on the debt owed to us, it wouldn't erase the original wound. The hurt, once it is enacted, is permanent. We must live with the unfairness and the sorrow of having our heart broken for the rest of our lives. Yes, remorse from the perpetrator helps, and yes, compensation makes the future a little easier to bear. But we will forever carry the wound within us. Even if the relationship with our perpetrator is restored, the damage done cannot be undone. This doesn't mean that we will remain a victim. Only if we remain unconscious and refuse to suffer what is ours to suffer will we act like a victim.

This might explain the brilliance and resonance of Leonard Cohen's "Hallelujah," a wildly popular song, I think because Cohen got right to the bone with it, both lyrically and melodically.

> *Love is not a victory march,*
> *it's a cold, and it's a broken hallelujah.*

I've presided at hundreds of wedding ceremonies over the years. Probably a dozen times the happy couple walked down the aisle to this song. Had they listened to the words? The song describes King David's lustful meeting with Bathsheba. The subtext is that to consummate his love, he has ordered Bathsheba's husband, a general in the army, to lead the charge in the next battle — ensuring his death. Any love that David and Bathsheba enjoy will be forever tinged by this act of violence. And once we've suffered heartbreak and/or violence enacted against us, our love will take on the feel of a broken hallelujah. It's not that we will never love again. But it will be textured. The hallelujahs we sing will be mixed with sadness and sorrow. It will be forever more like "Hallelujah anyhow."

Life isn't fair. There's no use arguing with that reality. Life is life. You get what you get. Human beings hurt other innocent human beings. It hurts, but nothing I do will change the truth of this. The creative response, once this is accepted, is to take an oath to never consciously cause suffering.

There's No Escaping It

This brings me to the third principle I learned on the mountain: There is no escaping it. We must face the suffering and accept it. All that is left to do is to suffer what is yours to suffer. For nine ceremonies in a row I ended up at the same heartbroken place. I was being shown that I needed to accept it. I saw that my suffering now was self-inflicted because I couldn't or wouldn't accept it.

The medicine was trying to get me to see two things: first, that I was living my life, in terms of my outlook and orientation, as if what happened was the only thing that ever happened to me. As long as I refused to accept it and suffer it, it would feel as though life was nothing but suffering. I finally understood that it was okay to have a broken heart but not okay for my broken heart to have me — that is, to colonize my whole personality. And it was definitely not okay to hurt others unconsciously because of my sorrow.

The second thing I saw was that much of my life was wasted as I tried to distract myself from this sorrow with alcohol, TV and a mind that would not shut off or shut up. I was never a raging addict, but I was always what I called a "low-grade junkie" in a song I wrote early in my career.

> *I'm just a low-grade junkie*
> *underneath this preacher's gown.*
> *I ain't nobody special*
> *and there ain't no good news going down.*
>
> *It's one more cup of coffee, two more Tylenol,*
> *a rum and coke and a TV show*
> *will help me to forget it all.*

Even my career choice, becoming a minister of religion, was a distraction from the main event. It was an attempt to solve the "problem" of the lack of meaning in my life. But as I'll share in the next chapter, it wasn't meaning that had gone missing but rather loving connection. When this is absent, life loses its meaning.

Takers

Ironically, we try to escape the third principle, which states that there is no escaping. One strategy many of us adopt is to try to redeem our own suffering by taking from the world, from relationships, from Earth whatever we damn well please — because the world owes us!

If we refuse as adults to suffer what is ours to suffer, we become net takers from life. My hunch is that this is why the Western, developed nations are net takers from the planet and from each other. Psychological, emotional and physical trauma, as we've seen, is more widespread than we admit. But repression and denial keep it buried. This means it comes out in other ways. The implicit violence of being net takers manifests as the presumed right to devastate the planet without guilt, the right to take without giving back in relationships, the right to be an asshole, the right to be selfish, the right to accumulate vast amounts of wealth in the midst of so much poverty, the right to take shortcuts, the right to be miserable, cynical and pessimistic. All these are ways of taking back what was taken from us when we didn't have a fighting chance.

I noticed a few years ago that as a net taker I was not a grateful person. It's impossible to feel that life owes you something and to be grateful at the same time. Deep gratitude is born of humility, which arises from a felt sense that we come into this world already on the receiving end of overwhelming abundance. In the ayahuasca ceremonies, much of my purging was simply getting rid of the taker within me.

On the mountain I saw that the universe is like a big mama's breast; when we're finished with one breast, there's another one on the other side ready to fill us. But if we don't feel this in our bones, we operate from the myth of insufficiency. Trauma causes us to feel that there is not enough for us, and that the only way to get enough is to become takers. When we are not adequately mothered, we become pathologically self-mothering. We learn that we cannot depend on anybody else or anything else to get by. We believe that the only thing that is coming our way is what we can take, or make happen, ourselves. We don't see how much comes to us freely and generously.

Gratitude as Spiritual Health

Gratitude, by definition, is the sense that everything is a gift and we are on the receiving end of generosity. All we have to do is show up. If we feel gratitude, we want to give back. Our whole life becomes a grateful response. But if we feel we're owed something, we become vampires, living off the life force of others. Sometimes this is confused with love.

Absence of gratitude is the premier sign of spiritual sickness. Something has gone terribly wrong if we don't walk around uttering thank-yous on a daily basis. Thank you, earth and minerals; thank you, air; thank you, sun and moon; thank you, animals and plants. When we adopt a taker stance, gratitude is the first casualty. Poet e.e. cummings was overwhelmed with gratitude when he wrote this poem:

I thank you god

for most this amazing day
for the leaping greenly spirits
and the blue true dream of sky.
and for everything that is natural,
that is infinite,
that is yes.
I who had died, am alive again today,
and this is the sun's birthday,
and the birth day of life, and of love
and wings
and of the gay, great happening
illimitably earth...

Paradoxically, it is in coming to terms with the three principles — life is suffering, it isn't fair, and there's no escaping it — that gratitude returns for all that is good and true and beautiful.

What I discovered was that once I truly accepted the three principles, the pressure to forgive lifted. If the purpose of forgiveness is to release us from the past by breaking the ties of resentment, we can accomplish the same thing by suffering what is ours to suffer and then letting it go.

This may be what many people mean when they say they have forgiven a perpetrator. They are no longer looking for the debt to be repaid. Peace has been restored. How did they get there? They suffered what was theirs to suffer.

The Son of Man Must Suffer

We take Jesus's teaching about forgiveness very seriously but ignore his teaching about suffering. He repeatedly told his disciples that the "son of man" (the True Human) must suffer and die. In other words, even the archetypal Human doesn't get to do an end run around the passivities. It's an inescapable feature of being human. Peter protested Jesus's announcement that even one as innocent as he must suffer, and Jesus rebuked him: "Get thee behind me, Satan." Strong words. The Satan is the one who tempts us away from our true path, and any true path will involve suffering.

Jesus, following in the steps of the suffering servant from the book of Isaiah, is having none of it. One way to understand Jesus's death is that God redeems humanity by identifying with the suffering of humanity through Jesus. Once we accept that life is suffering, it is not fair, and there is no escaping, we may discover that we've let our resentment, our anger and our debt go. This doesn't mean that we are obliged to be friends with, or even to like, our perpetrators. And if our perpetrator is not asking for forgiveness, it makes no sense to say that we've forgiven them. We have simply suffered their violence, learned from it and moved on.

Forgiveness as Transaction

Authentic forgiveness is an exchange between at least two people: a victim and a perpetrator. It is not a unilateral declaration by the victim.

The Jewish rabbi interviewed by Daan van Kampenhout in *The Tears of the Ancestors* outlines the five conditions that the perpetrator must fulfill in a gesture of authentic forgiveness:

1. He must admit that the crime happened, and that he is guilty.
2. He must say he is sorry.
3. He must admit that he has created or caused damage.
4. He must commit to making amends, and he must actually do so.
5. He must promise that he will never do it again.

Chloe Madanes, a family therapist in the United States, has a protocol for working with sexual abuse victims and their abusers that has similar steps but is perhaps more rigorous. On rare occasions a father will admit his abusive behavior to, for example, a daughter. Madanes will get him to ask for her forgiveness. But before the daughter responds, Madanes intervenes to make sure she feels her father's sincerity. I have heard that she will ask the father to get down on his knees to make his confession and express remorse. Madanes knows that the daughter will instinctively jump to forgive him because she is still in a position of dependency on him. Only after the daughter believes that her father is sincere will she be asked again if she forgives him. Madanes makes clear that, even in these circumstances, she is under no pressure to forgive him, and forgiveness might take a very long time, if it ever happens.

I once asked Malidoma Somé, an African elder and author, what his own people, the Dagara tribe in Burkina Faso, teach about forgiveness. He said that there was no direct teaching about forgiveness. (I have trouble imagining this, given how central the concept is in the Christian West.) Instead, the Dagara are taught ways to allow their body to soften after being hurt by another person. They know intuitively that the only way for a body to soften is to grieve — that is, to suffer and let it go. They have many grieving rituals. But we in the West have forgotten that grief is a natural part of life. The refusal to grieve produces a hardened body, and a hardened body is correlated with violence. The art of living consists in keeping a soft body in a harsh world.

Life is suffering. But I want to be clear that life is also a lot more than suffering. Once we've faced the suffering that we couldn't face when we were too young to integrate it, we can let it go. The only suffering we truly hold on to is the suffering that remains unconscious and unexpressed. Once it has surfaced, we can develop a relationship with it. If we have a relationship with it, we are no longer *identified* with it. It is *part* of our story, not the whole story. After we've done our work, we can be open to the full range of life's possibilities — including joy, ecstasy, love, awe, reverence and gratitude. We suffer what is ours to suffer not as an end in itself but to gain the capacity to see and feel the intrinsic beauty of life.

CHAPTER 9

The Search for Meaning

People say that what we're all seeking is the meaning of life. I don't think that's what we're really seeking. I think what we're seeking is an experience of being alive.

— **Joseph Campbell**

I Think, Therefore I Am?

I've taken 300 micrograms of LSD. My therapist is holding me. I'm looking into his eyes and feeling intense love.

Then, out of nowhere, I split off and start thinking about life. I mean, obsessively thinking. Which is weird. I am playing out a memory — replicating the experience of intense love and how I cut myself off, anticipating being hurt. Isolating myself like this is no fun, but it is apparently more tolerable than the alternative.

In this condition, having cut myself off from relationship, the question of the meaning of life emerges. I want to know what is real and true. I want to know how I can trust what I think is real and true. How do I know, and what can I know? Philosophically, these are the questions of ontology and epistemology. But experientially it just feels like intense cerebral activity. On the LSD, I set myself the task to capture the essence of life in two fundamental principles. I'm not sure why it's just two, but that is the task.

The intensity of my thinking matches the intensity of love I felt at the beginning of the session, except this is not pleasurable. I have pretty much lost track of the other human being in the room. And the medicine is showing me how I compensated for needing to cut off from an unsafe relationship. I shifted away from the experience of life into thinking *about* life. I see the solipsistic nature of my thinking, circling back on myself. I watch myself create a complete metaphysical system.

After I painstakingly construct my philosophy around the two foundational principles, I turn to my therapist and ask him to grab a pen. I'm about to drop the mother lode on him. I get him to lean in, and then I laugh: "I got you, didn't I? You actually believed I would deliver on the meaning of life."

I don't have a clue whether he is interested or not. I am projecting onto him the part of me that truly believes I will find redemption and meaning through my intellect. This experience with LSD makes a mockery of that conviction, which I have clung to for so many years. The session is nothing less than the dethroning of my intellectual strategy.

I think it is terribly funny. As in the myth of Sisyphus, the philosopher's stone rolls all the way back down to the bottom and I start over. I push the stone up the hill again until I arrive at my new and improved version of truth, only to lose control at the last minute and watch the stone bounce away from me once more. In the session I repeat this cycle at least four times.

I barf. It is truly sickening what I'm doing, what I've done my whole life. I am trapped in my own thoughts and unable to escape.

I think of the famous dictum of philosopher and mathematician René Descartes. He was trying to sort out for himself what was real and whether *he* was real and finally decided that "I think, therefore I am." He introduced radical skepticism as a way to defeat skepticism about God on its own grounds. Doubt everything. Doubt even that God wouldn't arbitrarily change the nature of reality itself once we arrived at a truth. God, he surmised, might be the Great Deceiver. Not only might God deceive me that something is true when it's not. God might take something that was indeed true up until this moment in time and then change the world — and do it over and over again.

Everything else, he continued, other than my own thoughts, was created outside of me. Thought alone is internally generated. I can trust that my thoughts are real. And if there is an "I" to be deceived, then "I" must at least exist.

If this is starting to make you feel dizzy, then you know how I felt. If I didn't know that acid wasn't created until the 1940s, I'd swear that René was tripping.

Well, sure, I think to myself. René, you can know that you exist because you think. But, dude, why are you questioning your existence in the first place?

Descartes's mother died when he was a year old. He was sent to live with his grandmother. He was sickly as a child, and illness persisted through his life. It's impossible to know how the absence of maternal affection affected his philosophy. But I do know that if we aren't seen and celebrated at this developmental stage, we question our very existence. Babies and toddlers need an "other" to confirm their reality by acting as a mirror and empathizing with them. If this doesn't happen, a self will not form. The child who does not see herself in her mother's or father's eyes will spend the rest of her life in search of a self and in search of meaning.

Contact, Not Content

I pick myself up off the floor, wipe up my vomit, then turn back to my therapist and say, "Andrew, it's a New Order. You can't think your way to what's real and true."

"True" has nothing to do with propositional truth. True, in the sense that I mean it, is more like a degree of intensity, undeniable in depth yet ineffable. It's a *feeling* of connection with self and other. As Joseph Campbell said, it's a feeling of being alive. By "New Order" I mean that I see it is necessary for me to make a quantum leap into a new paradigm. Mine isn't working. And then I turn to him and say:

It's contact, not content!

Over and over I come back to this revelation. Contact, not content. "Content" is my thoughts about the nature of reality — the complex metaphysics I was creating with my disconnected intellect. "Contact" means just that. The only way I can know what is real and true — that *I* am real and true — is through contact with another, a safe, loving connection. I had absolutely no interest in abstract conceptualization when I was in contact with my therapist at the beginning of the session. It was only after splitting off, because of fear, that I started ruminating about the meaning of life and how I could know if I was real and what was true.

TM or Jesus?

What happened in this session was nothing new. I had been what one author calls a "meaning freak" since my early twenties. I wasn't a great student in high school or during my undergraduate degree. I got by, but my main interest was sports. I was a good athlete. I attended the university that had the best volleyball team in Canada and got an undergraduate degree in psychology at the same time. But something happened in my final year. I became obsessed by the question of the meaning of life. This obsession came out of the blue. My grades were average until I found a course called Transcendental Psychology. I aced the course. I started to meditate.

My jock friends wondered what was up with Sanguin. In the Introduction I described how I was on the verge of taking an advanced course in TM (Transcendental Meditation) when I was "saved" by Jesus. I attended an evangelical rally where the preacher spoke about Jesus as "the way, the truth and the life." I had become a meaning freak, and if Jesus was the way, the truth and the life, then why not give him a shot?

I went through the rigmarole of giving my life to Jesus. And I have to say, despite some embarrassment in retrospect, that something happened. I experienced unconditional love. I remember falling in love with every person I saw on the street. I poured all my booze down the sink. And I married the woman I was living with. I couldn't believe it. So this was what everybody was talking about when they spoke of love! I truly had never experienced it.

I started attending church again after a long hiatus. One Sunday the minister called me into his office after the service. He sat across from me, smoking his pipe, and declared that as far as he could tell I had only three options for a career: doctor, lawyer or minister.

Huh?! He was the first person in my life who had ever suggested that I could be anything other than a Zamboni driver, cleaning the ice between periods of the hockey game for the City of Winnipeg. I took him seriously. I figured that since Jesus was "the way," it was a no-brainer. The minister handed me an application form for seminary in Toronto. Why this man stocked seminary application forms in his office is beyond me.

My wife and I packed what there was to pack, which wasn't much, and headed to Toronto. I started seminary that fall. I loved the heady climate. I fell in love with books. I had a lot of catching up to do. In the second year I discovered that they gave out money for top grades — good money on a student's budget. Between my wife's work as a flight attendant, scholarships, my part-time work waiting tables, and loads of caffeine, we got through these years.

With six months to go before ordination, I freaked out. It had never occurred to me that I was actually preparing myself to lead a congregation. I was there to figure out the meaning of life. Everybody else was talking about the importance of "community." I didn't have a clue what they were on about. I was deep into theology and philosophy, and with a one-year-old to feed and a job at night slinging food, community was not high on my list of priorities. I was into content, not contact! I deferred ordination to train in psychotherapy. But my hunch is that the purpose of this training was less about preparing myself to see clients and more a chance to continue gnawing away at the meaning of life.

The Well-Cooked Omelet

After my second year of seminary I was required to do an internship. I moved my small family to Milton, Ontario. Thus began my practical education. But I still had my head buried in books.

I remember having lunch at the Acorn Café on Main Street, an egg salad sandwich. I read a poem, the last line of which was "the meaning of life is the tear of joy shed at the sight of a well-cooked omelet." I have no memory of paying the bill. I felt like I was lifted up off the ground and carried down Main Street. Everything was in slow motion. I cannot remember my feet touching the ground. I ended up in a field of wheat on the outskirts of town. The autumn sun lit up the heads of wheat blowing in the wind. I was in ecstasy. Everything was flow. Everything was connected. The line between me and what I was seeing blurred. My prayer was that this bliss would never end. Which, of course, marked its end.

Ecstasy literally means "out of the place where we stand." The ecstasy of this experience was that it brought needed relief from my feeling of separation and disconnection. The "place where we stand" is the adapted self and its insatiable need to appropriate everything to itself so we can assure ourselves that we really do exist. To be relieved of that self and to make direct contact with the world was pure bliss. I was also given a glimpse of the extraordinary glory shining through and manifesting as the physical world.

I've spent decades trying to understand why this very simple line of poetry would trigger a mystical experience. As well as enabling me to stand outside myself and unselfconsciously unite with a wheat field, my guess is it was an invitation to *feel* life, not just think about it. I made contact.

Giving Up the Big Map of Everything

Big Ideas have always attracted me. The bigger the Map of Everything the better. It's why I was so engrossed by the works of lay philosopher Ken Wilber. His integral theory attempted to exclude nothing (i.e., include everything) from his map of reality. I am in debt to Wilber. His system is for geeks who get off on locating everything and everybody on the map. Ken cautions against confusing the map with the territory, but, in practice, everybody ends up falling in love with the map, forgetting that the territory is more complex, nuanced and mysterious than any philosophical system.

These days, when I see long threads on Facebook where people are arguing endlessly, and in nuanced detail, about metaphysical truth, I'm not interested. There was a time when I couldn't resist weighing in. Now I wonder if what these folks are truly looking for is contact. But they are trying to get contact through content.

When I was in the therapy session on LSD, I pantomimed this obsessive intellectual search for meaning by mimicking masturbation. Not a one-hander. Both arms stretched around a penis the size of a tree and I was giving 'er. In retrospect, it was the perfect gesture. Obsessive intellectualizing is such a solitary, solipsistic activity. If we don't make contact with an other, we will never escape chronic self-involvement. We're just wanking. The mind loops back on itself. But what we're trying to escape is this self-enclosed mind and the identity that forms around ceaseless, purpose-less thought.

There Is an Other. I Care.

I wept. My mind hadn't been able to figure it out. But what came next felt like a revelation from Source. Some higher mind revealed it to me, and, ironically, in exactly two principles! There is an Other. I Care.

That was it. The New Order, to which all my subsequent thinking would be in service.

I saw the other in the eyes of my therapist. And I saw that this other cared. His otherness was absolute to me, as was mine to him. But we bridged that absolute otherness with love. He cared. He saw me. This, I realized, was the only way to know the truth that I was real. Descartes may have gained intellectual satisfaction, but was he in truth looking for an other who cared and who saw him? I'd change Descartes's famous dictum to *I connect, therefore I am.* This is what Thich Nhat Hanh meant by inter-being: "I am through you, so I."

My wife came to sit with me at the end of the session. I was very high. I tried to tell her of how heartbreaking it was to care. It was like this epic journey, I told her, across a universe of resistance. The way I coped with not being loved was to stop caring, or at least to pretend I didn't care. Now "I," the caring me, was coming back online, and there wasn't much left to do but grieve.

It was so simple and obvious that I had missed it. I missed it because I formed a belief very early in my life that it was too painful to take in the other, and too painful to care. I couldn't bear it.

It was this second principle that broke me open. I care. I saw that it might not have happened this way, and that most of the world proceeds without care for the other. This is what people mean when they talk about "othering" the other. We see the absolute otherness of the other, but we don't care about them. We "other" them, and then the other becomes a threat to us. We dehumanize them and have done so for millennia. This is the history of violence in a nutshell. But this is pathological "othering."

New age spirituality tries to counter this violent tendency by denying the absolute otherness of the other, making the romantic claim that "we are all one." I get it. Reality is interconnection. It's true that we are all re-configured expressions of the Great Flaring Forth, in human form after 13.8 billion years of evolution; we're made from stardust; we are concentrated amalgams of everything that preceded us, yes. But the universe is not *only* a communion event. Differentiation needs to be held in tension with unity. We are unique, irreducible manifestations of the evolutionary process. I am a genuine other to you, as you are to me.

New age spirituality privileges unity, "oneness" and non-duality over otherness and individuality in reaction to the violence of treating others as objects. But the problem isn't with radical individuality. In fact, radical individuality is what the universe is aiming at. The problem is that when we "other" humans without caring, we dehumanize them, and we are then free to treat them as "its" and not "thous," as Jewish philosopher Martin Buber has phrased it.

I was disturbed to discover how I pretended to stop caring in response to trauma. Pretending to stop caring is a defense against suffering. I say "pretending" because my heart never truly stopped caring. Underneath apparent indifference, armor, easy-go-lucky facades or nothing-affects-me posturing was a heart that never stopped caring.

I learned to separate myself to survive and then started looking for meaning. But meaning is not hiding under a rock somewhere. It's every-where, if we're willing to first feel it and connect with it. It's in the relationships we cultivate with humans, plants, animals, the air, the water and with Source. In fact, I didn't need to find meaning. I was just starved for connection. I traveled north into my cerebral cortex; I had to figure it all out because I couldn't feel it. In my obsessive need to substitute content for connection, I couldn't escape me. This is my new definition of hell.

Isolation proved to be a poor strategy. It took a lifetime to realize it. The only way back to my humanity, the only way to figure it all out, was to suffer the grief of lost years and start over. That line of poetry changed my life. But it took thirty years to integrate.

CHAPTER 10

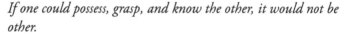

There Is an Other, and I Care

If one could possess, grasp, and know the other, it would not be other.

— **Emmanuel Levinas**

The Hegemonic Self

This chapter is different from the others. It isn't a reflection on an ayahuasca ceremony or a psychedelic psychotherapy session. It's an account of deepening a psychedelic experience through conscious integration. The integration is as critical as the experience of the ayahuasca. It's the difference between having just another psychedelic experience and transformation.

After the journey, described in the last chapter, my therapist pointed me toward a twentieth-century Jewish philosopher, Emmanuel Levinas. I'd never heard of him, but when I looked into his work, it felt synchronistic to me. His entire philosophy organizes around the two principles that I had arrived at: there is an other, and I care.

Talk about bone on bone! Levinas challenges the whole philosophical tradition, from Parmenides to Heidegger, which asserts that meaning is found through thought or reason. Not so, says he. These philosophical systems are self-enclosed and self-enclosing. They are hegemonic in their attempt to colonize reality and reduce its complexity, nuance and enigma — including human reality — to a system of thought.

This reduction, which begins and ends with the self, he calls "the Same," following Plato. What he means is that, left to its own devices, the self will appropriate, engulf and incorporate the whole of reality to itself. This he calls the "totality." Sameness reduces everything to sameness. At the heart of all totalitarian regimes, ideologies and bad religions is this impulse for totality. Everything is assimilated into a comprehensive unity or whole. He notes how often "regimes of charity," from Christianity to Marxism to Communism, become regimes of violence because of this hegemonic tendency to both ignore and discourage difference and otherness.

This resonated for me as I remembered that what was so painful about my intellectual trip was that I couldn't get outside myself. Everything ended up being referred to "me." Yet it was this me I was trying to transcend. According to Levinas, what philosophy doesn't show us is that we will never find primary meaning in thought, because thought belongs to this realm of totality. Only the presence of the infinite, breaking in, breaking through and breaking down the order of this insatiable self, can liberate us.

The Infinite in the Face of the Other

By "infinite" Levinas doesn't mean God although what he describes sure feels like what theologians mean by God. For him, the infinite is the enigmatic face of the absolutely other human breaking into the order of the Same and overturning it. This vulnerable and destitute other has infinite need of us. This infinite need is the "face" of the other.

The infinite is necessarily from the "outside." It cannot come from within the order of the Same. Otherwise, the smallness and inadequacy of this order, the totality, would never be revealed. The other precedes us. In fact, in Levinas's philosophy, the other is the bedrock of reality. The other makes the world — including language and the capacity to think abstractly about life — possible. This is why Levinas speaks of ethics as philosophy and metaphysics. How we treat each other is the ground of both. Language, abstract thought and the self should rightly be put in service of the infinite. It is the absolute other that redirects abstract thinking, shapes the way we frame reality and talk about it with others, and enlarges the small self by connecting it with what is ultimately true and good.

Levinas claims that the "face" of the other is devastating. By "face" he doesn't mean actual features, the eyes, nose, ears and mouth. He means the enigmatic, naked and vulnerable presence that both pleads with us in its vulnerable state and possesses an authority we are forced to contend with. If we ignore the vulnerability and the authoritative summons, even our willful ignoring is evidence of the claim that the other has already made on our life.

The presence of the other disrupts the ego's appropriation of the world to itself and explodes totality. After I had sickened myself by intellectually wanking my way through four complete metaphysical systems, I looked up at my therapist and saw an other. I vacillated between an astonished query: "There is an other?" and a declaration: "There is an other!" This was at once a discovery, a relief and a summons to come out of my isolation and into relationship.

For Levinas, there is no reciprocity in relationship. The other is privileged over self. The fact of the other was a summons to come out of my bubble of isolation, to care. But remember, we too are the "other" to others.

Thou Shalt Not Kill

The otherness of the other is absolute for Levinas. This otherness cannot be obliterated by our ego, by political ideologies or by false religions, because it is more fundamental. This is because the other is not just another idea. The other is beyond ideation.

The other obliterates us. That is, it obliterates our totalizing impulse.

In his writing and in interviews, Levinas refers frequently to a scene in a novel by the Russian novelist and journalist Valerie Grossman. In *Life and Fate,* Grossman describes a scene in which the Russians have just defeated the German siege on Stalingrad. German prisoners are recruited to clean up the carnage. A young German is going about his task and comes upon a teenage girl who was murdered in the siege. An old woman sees the despair in his eyes and enjoys it. She hates this German. She picks up a brick and walks toward him, fully intending to smash his face with it.

But when she is close enough to him, she reaches into her pocket and offers him a precious piece of bread. Later, the old woman reflects on the experience and judges herself a fool. She does not know what possessed her.

Levinas writes: "In the innocence of our daily lives, the face of the other signifies above all a demand. The face requires you, calls you outside. And already there resounds the word from Sinai, 'Thou shalt not kill,' which signifies that you shall defend the life of the other…It is the very articulation of love of the other. You are indebted to someone from whom you have not borrowed a thing. And you are responsible, the only one who could answer, the noninterchangeable and unique one…In this relation of the unique to the unique there appears…the original sociality."

According to Levinas, the old woman saw the "face" of this German soldier in his vulnerability and felt summoned to care, to choose love over hate. This summoning was more powerful than her ego. It called her "out" — that is, outside of her totalizing self. The "original sociality" is the choice to let the German soldier be — to not kill him.

The commandment "Thou shalt not kill" was not arbitrarily imposed upon the Jews by some priest who thought it was a good strategy to keep the community from killing each other. It was a phenomenological reality, evoked in and through the experience of the other. The old Russian woman discovers the existential nature of this commandment when she is about to smash the German's face with the brick. She discovers an a priori ethical impulse that is built into the foundations of being human. This ethical impulse can be ignored, but, as mentioned, to override it is to acknowledge its preexisting imperative. She is surprised to discover that the "face" of the German soldier possesses the power to summon her deep humanity.

At the bone-deep level of reality, every interaction we have with every "other" in the course of our life requires that we make a fundamental, if unconscious, decision not to kill that other — to let them be. But to let the other be means that the other exerts authority over us in its essential mortal condition. To let the other be requires that we relinquish our life of enjoyment (although, for Levinas, enjoyment is good and necessary) and, to use the biblical images that Levinas is fond of, "feed the hungry, care for the widow and orphan, clothe the naked."

In the Bible, God is the wholly Other (according to theologian Karl Barth), who breaks in and disrupts the order of the world. But the vessels for this divine disruption are more often than not the widow, the orphan, the imprisoned, the hungry and the naked. In the New Testament, Jesus clarified that if you want contact with God, you turn your life inside out for the most vulnerable. "Inasmuch as you have done it unto the least of these, you have done it unto me."

The effect of generational trauma is precisely that it causes men and women, mothers and fathers, sons and daughters to ignore the commandment to not kill. It renders invisible the vulnerable and naked "face" of the other. We metaphorically kill off our children when we cannot see their "face." In that refusal to see the other, we refuse the in-breaking of the infinite. We refuse what is ultimately true and real, and we ourselves are reduced to taking from the world, appropriating even our own children into our "sameness." We feed off them, as we feed off the whole world, to bolster our ego, when we should instead acknowledge and celebrate their absolute otherness because it places us under an infinite responsibility.

When we cannot allow our own vulnerability because of trauma, the moment we see vulnerability in the face of the other, we revolt. We cut ourselves off from the other's pain because it reminds us of what is just below the surface in our lives. It's only when we have learned to accept our own suffering, born in trauma, that we gain the capacity to have our ego overthrown by the suffering of others.

The meaning of life is revealed not through intellectual content but through contact with absolute others in their naked vulnerability. As Levinas asserts, because the need of others is infinite, an infinite and impossible generosity is summoned from us in return. We don't choose this. The face of the other, the infinite, disrupts our life. It comes to us from outside our meaning system. The other chooses us.

The Miracle of Caring

We underestimate what a miracle it is to care. Most of our life consists of politeness, being cordial and exchanging pleasantries. These are at once concealing and revealing the deeper truth buried in our ingrained habits of sociality. The deeper meaning of these pleasantries is that we have decided a) to let the other be (that is, to not kill), and b) we are responsible to the other and for the other. This isn't conscious, but when it becomes conscious we incur an impossible responsibility. The other's claim on us precedes and trumps our right to perpetuate the world of self. But for Levinas, this new responsibility is not a burden. It elevates us. The other is "high and lifted up," to borrow a biblical phrase describing God (Isaiah 57:15).

In seeing this and allowing the in-breaking infinite to reorder our lives, we discover our own dignity. In the newly found responsibility that the face of the vulnerable other has imposed on us, we discover our deep humanity. We are, Levinas says, "elected" or called — like the Jews. But this election is not for privilege. It is to serve, not so much "the world" (for the world is too impersonal, too universal, for Levinas) but rather the unique individual before us who makes a claim on us in his or her naked vulnerability.

It's important to note that while Levinas privileges the other over the totalizing impulse of the self, this doesn't mean that love of self is unhealthy. The self that appropriates all experiences of the other in order to feel substantial is the traumatized self. But to "love our neighbour as our self," as Jesus puts it, requires that we are able to approach our own vulnerable self as an other needing to be protected, nurtured and nourished. In the next chapter I will share my first authentic experience of self-love, which happened on an ayahuasca journey.

CHAPTER 11

Love of Self

Self-love, my liege, is not so vile a sin as self-neglect.
— **Shakespeare**, *Henry V*

I Am Not Bad

When I was twenty-eight, training as a psychotherapist, I entered bioenergetic therapy. This is a body-oriented school of therapy founded by Alexander Lowen. The therapist reads and releases trauma that is stored in the body as bands of contracted muscles. As muscles release, trauma surfaces.

In one session I was lying in a fetal position. I looked up at my therapist and out of nowhere announced "I am not bad." This surprised me. I was a good guy, a nice guy. Good was kind of my MO. There was no conscious part of myself that believed I was bad. So where was this protest coming from, and to whom was it directed?

As I allowed the voice to have its say, it became increasingly vociferous. I Am Not Bad.

Turns out this feeling of being bad is not uncommon. Emotional trauma causes it. Psychologist Robert Firestone writes: "The child must conceptualize himself as bad or unlovable in order to defend against the realization that the parents are inadequate. Recognition of the real faults in the parent would destroy the bond, or the imagined connection."[21]

I am not bad. Underneath this protest, what I really wanted to say was "*You* are bad. *You* fucked up." This was the lost voice of two- or three-year-old me, finally feeling safe enough with a therapist to verbalize what was unspeakable in my early years.

The sad irony is that even though we form this unconscious belief that we are bad (to protect the image of our parents as good), God help the person who corroborates it with feedback, or even an innocent hint, that suggests we really *are* bad!

This unconscious belief that I was bad was triggered whenever somebody offered what they considered to be constructive feedback. But to me, they were seeing right through me, into my badness. The information they were offering about their experience of me elicited an unconscious protest that was directed not at them but at my mother by a devastated toddler.

When I was that toddler, I was made to feel like I was rotten to the core. I felt inadequate in the face of my mother's need for me to be a certain way for her, and I felt fear that because of my inadequacy I was going to be on the receiving end of her rage. To this day a woman's needs trigger fears that I cannot meet them, and that if I don't meet them I'm going to be hurt. When I couldn't meet a need, it confirmed my secret belief that there was something wrong with me. But my only "flaw" was that I couldn't be what my mother needed me to be. I couldn't face that truth, because if I couldn't be all that she needed me to be, I believed that she wouldn't be able to take care of me. My survival was at stake. Because I intuitively sensed her fragility, I believed that my demands and feelings might destroy her. Then where would I be?

When my daughter tried to tell me how much I had hurt her by leaving her mother when she was two, I responded in a similar way. I simply wouldn't hear it. To my shame, I tried to get her to see "reason." I couldn't see that I was merely defending myself against my unconscious belief that I was bad and that I was inadequate. My reasons didn't matter to her. That

---

21   Robert Firestone, *The Fantasy Bond: The Structure of Psychological Defenses* (New York: Human Sciences Press, 1985), 41.

her mother absconded with her to a city 1,500 miles from where I lived didn't matter. Nor did it matter that her mother actively obstructed our relationship. What she needed me to hear was that I had left. I had hurt her. She had her own story to tell. My narcissistic wound kept me from hearing her.

Thank god for the medicine. My daughter came and joined me in an ayahuasca ceremony, after which I apologized for how I had hurt her. I asked her forgiveness. Once you die to your ego, there are more important things in life than maintaining your illusion of perfection. But this only became possible after I had worked through my trauma.

Love of self is a precondition for loving others. New age spirituality got this part right. But what many new age spiritual teachers fail to see is that we cannot love ourselves until we deal with trauma. Trauma, as I've said, is a failure of love. Under stress we will default to assuming we are bad. If we've made a mistake, we will default to this unconscious belief. It's futile to badger a person to love herself when this unconscious belief is still in place.

In my experience with clients, I find this unconscious feeling of being bad underneath a veneer of good behavior is pervasive. It explains why so many of us treat ourselves so badly and why self-sabotage is a chronic condition. Why are we so able to be compassionate with others when we unleash the furies of hell on ourselves if we make mistakes? We learned early to expect no quarter when dealing with our own mistakes and missteps.

In one ceremony I saw a vision of an abandoned newborn in the back of a gutted car in an industrial park. It was a cold and pathetic backdrop. I was handed this little baby, who was now mine to care for. I was being summoned to parent myself. This is not the same as what Firestone means by self-mothering, which is the adamant and rigorous refusal to receive any support. I needed and received much support in the healing process. But healing doesn't start until we take responsibility for loving the abused little one within.

Until we feel self-compassion, we will internalize the critical voice of the parent(s) who hurt us. We will hurt ourselves rather than love ourselves.

My Amazing Body

Lying there in the maloca, after multiple rounds of purging, I feel com-passion for myself in a way I have never experienced. I scan my entire body. My feet are cold. I speak to my feet with surprising tenderness: *Oh, you're so cold. Here, let me warm you up.*

A memory surfaces of my father rubbing my freezing feet between periods of a hockey game, played outside in Winnipeg in -35 degree C weather.

As I continue my scan, I stop at every injury I incurred playing sports. There was the concussion I suffered when I was around twelve playing tackle football. I was small for my age, and this monster fullback who played for River Heights kneed me in the head. I made the tackle, but I was almost knocked out. I stayed in the game. The fullback came up to me after the game and congratulated me on being fearless. I paid for that apparent fearlessness. In the ceremony, I hold my head where his knee hit my helmet and apologize to my twelve-year-old self for putting him through that.

Another concussion occurred on the basketball court when I fell hard on the knee of a defender and broke my cheekbone. I was in bed for a few days, throwing up. I put my hand over my eye in a healing gesture.

I stop at my left shoulder. I'm left-handed, and I strained that shoulder to the breaking point — throwing baseballs and footballs, shooting bas-ketballs, spiking in volleyball, falling off my bike as an adult, lifting weights. I lay my hands on my shoulder, offering healing touch and grati-tude that this part of my body never received. It's strange to say, but I had never thought to thank my body for getting me through so well.

Then my toes, which I broke playing volleyball, and my ankles, which I repeatedly sprained.

I stop the scan when I reach my heart and realize how it has faithfully circulated my blood and reoxygenated my body for almost sixty years. I have taken my heart for granted. This extends in my consciousness to all my bodily systems: respiratory, digestive, eliminatory, nervous, hormonal, etc. All of these systems I took for granted. I haven't cultivated a relationship with any of them. Biology class taught me these functions are "autonomic," so what was the point of gratitude? But without gratitude there can be no true respect, and no inquiry into how I can better support my body with proper nutrition, rest and exercise. I think of all the booze, caffeine and sugar I have dumped into my body. And still my body carries on.

For the first time in my life I love my body. I hold my hands up before my eyes and see how exquisite my fingers are. I touch each one with tenderness. Then I look at my feet and wiggle my toes. I remember playing with my daughter's toes when she was a baby.

I am falling in love with my embodied self. I realize that although I protested that I was not bad almost thirty-nine years earlier, because I never completed the inquiry into why I had formed that belief about myself, I have treated myself in the intervening years as though I didn't deserve respect or love. I stopped listening to my body.

What this meant practically is that I didn't stop to listen to what my body was telling me. I didn't respect my internal rhythms, which are trustworthy guides in telling me when to act and when to rest, when to make a move and when to be quiet and passive, what to eat, how much to eat, who to befriend and who to stay away from, and how to create safety for myself without judging whether or not I was able to handle certain people or circumstances.

Loving oneself means taking ourselves as seriously as we take others. It means we are actually free to not do anything in life that we don't truly want to do. "Endure nothing" is how my therapist puts it. We are under no obligation to live according to the expectations others may have of us or according to societal ideals of what is right and wrong, good or bad. We're under no obligation to spend time with people we don't want to spend time with. The invitation is to honour our own deepest feelings and intuitions, to access that furry little animal within, whose instincts are never wrong.

Narcissism: Healthy and Unhealthy

In the last chapter I wrote at some length about the need to get outside the self by taking in and responding to the vulnerable face of the other. And isn't love of self merely narcissism? But I think it's obvious from my description above that my love of my body in no way implies cutting off from love of the other. On the contrary, it is a precondition of loving the other.

It is important to distinguish between healthy narcissism and patho-logical narcissism. For the first few years of life, all children need to have their narcissistic needs met. They need to know that they are the center of the universe, and that nothing they can do will cause love to be withdrawn. This healthy narcissism consists of being seen and contained in one's full range of feelings towards parent(s) — all feelings, including envy, jealousy, rage, hatred, tenderness and sexual impulses. When these feelings and sen-sations are allowed free expression, with no shaming or embarrassment from the parent, we learn that our feelings and sensations, whatever they may be, are okay and are trustworthy.

If the mother or father were not themselves contained in their full range of feelings, they will not be able to tolerate these emotional expressions in the child. They will require the child to contain those feelings within him-self, to take care of the parent's need to not remember their own heartbreak and therefore to not feel those unacceptable feelings in himself. In this mi-lieu of non-containment and non-acceptance, the true self needs to hide. The false self begins the process of conforming to the poorly parented par-ent. The false self learns that its own needs, sensations and feelings are not safe to feel. But these constitute the very life of the budding self. Thus be-gins the process of deadening the sensations and feelings of the body.

Unhealthy narcissism is when an adult uses others to make up for this stunted sense of self. The empty space that was meant to be a self is insa-tiable. Such people will use others, including their own children, to fill the space. Narcissism turns the world into a mirror. The other exists solely to reflect and validate the unformed self. The tragedy is that such people will never be successful in their attempt to turn others into the mirror they never had as a child. Everything becomes about them and them alone. These people cannot love themselves because they are forever looking to others for confirmation of their existence and worth. Neither can they love others because others only exist to serve this underlying need.

Self as Other

The only way out is to deal with the original trauma, grieve the failure and then withdraw expectations that anyone outside us can fill the void. A therapist who is willing to hold us in our grief and offer unconditional love in the context of therapy can help. But in the end we need to internalize this support. We can learn to turn toward self with the same compassion and tenderness. This is genuine self-love, not narcissism.

It might help to imagine the self as an other who needs love. What if we treated our own vulnerability as an "other" who summons us, as Levinas suggests, and commands our care? This is what came online in the ceremony as I turned toward my neglected self with tenderness.

Seeing My Beauty

I am lying on my mat, feeling sorrowful but unable to release emotionally. This is a familiar condition for me on the medicine. I know that I need to let it out, but I have built up so much resistance over the years that I can't, or won't, let go.

I hear the voice of an assistant whispering to me that the shaman wants to work on me. I am escorted to him and invited to lie down. He lays his hands on my stomach and begins to chant. At one point, when his hands are on my left side just below my rib cage, I feel an energetic release. The terrible pain is gone and I begin to breathe deeply. When the healing is over I am taken back to my mat.

Within seconds I start to weep. I keel over at the end of my mat and begin to release all the stored emotion. Then the words come to me: *You are so beautiful, Bruce. You are so beautiful.*

This is not a contrived positive affirmation. Every cell of my body knows it to be true. It has the feel of objective truth. What is being communicated is that when we are born into the world we arrive with such a radiance and beauty.

William Wordsworth immortalized this feeling in his poem "Ode: Intimations of Immortality from Recollections of Early Childhood":

> *Our birth is but a sleep and a forgetting;*
> *The Soul that rises with us, our life's Star,*
> *Hath had elsewhere its setting,*
> *And cometh from afar:*
> *Not in entire forgetfulness,*
> *And not in utter nakedness,*

But trailing clouds of glory do we come
From God, who is our home:
Heaven lies about us in our infancy!

I always thought this was little more than romantic piffle. But now I feel it to be true. We are so beautiful when we come into the world.

And then come the words: *They didn't know how to do beautiful, Bruce. It wasn't your fault.*

The reason I express this in the passive voice is that the voice feels so foreign. Maybe it's from the "home" that Wordsworth alludes to, or maybe it's the voice of our lost soul. In any case, on the medicine it feels like I'm being *spoken to* with my own words. More tears.

I couldn't have thought this up with my logical mind in a thousand years. When I hear *They didn't know how to do beautiful, Bruce,* I realize that there are only two choices when faced with the "life star" of a newborn:

Amplify and celebrate his or her beauty.

Or

Reduce the voltage — find ways, that is, to remove the shine. That way you don't have to deal with your pain as a parent whose own beauty was diminished in childhood.

Welcome to the human race. We cannot deal with your radiance, so we will destroy it.

Does this sound far-fetched? To me it makes sense of the history of violence toward children. Humans have not reached the stage of evolution at which we consciously know that "the Soul that rises with us...hath had elsewhere its setting, and cometh from afar...trailing clouds of glory."

This was corroborated independently when I read Robert Firestone's book *The Fantasy Bond.* He describes the married couple as a partnership in which two people have agreed to not challenge the love equilibrium they have reached. This equilibrium (what I called a threshold in Chapter 3) is the highest degree of love they can respectively tolerate without becoming anxious — without, that is, their "fantasy bond" being challenged. The fantasy bond is their imagined, not actual, love for each other, a bond that reflects their imagined, not actual, love of their mothers for them. The fantasy bond is a psychological defense against the devastating reality that they were not adequately loved as children. If a child is born to this couple, the baby's helplessness and vulnerability challenges their defense (the fantasy bond), threatening to expose the truth that they were not loved adequately when they were helpless and dependent. The fantasy bond is thus passed on to the child. Another generation is born who will spend their lives defending themselves against the terrible absence of true love.

"In order to maintain their unreal ties, men and women must necessarily dull their real experiences and numb the aliveness of their children," Firestone writes. "The psychological equilibrium of the couple must not be disturbed by the intrusion of a spontaneous, lively, loving and affectionate child."[22]

Welcoming a Child: The Way of the Magi and the Way of Herod

The birth narrative of Jesus reflects this violence enacted against children in order to preserve "the kingdom" — in this case the kingdom of Herod, which is a political state of equilibrium that he does not want disrupted by a child.

The biblical story does not need to be literally true to be phenomenologically accurate. We are presented with two dramatically different ways of welcoming a child. There is the way of the Magi: discerning that a great and beautiful soul has been made incarnate, they come to pay homage and bring gifts. They want to amplify the child's beauty. Then there is Herod's way, representing the baser and far more common impulse of the human species: destroy him at all costs, thus ensuring that love does not disrupt the kingdom (or family).

The story of the gospels revolves around this same theme. Some follow Jesus as a divine incarnation. Others, those who are envious and resentful, plot to execute him.

I pray for the time when each one of us is seen, welcomed and celebrated for who we are — beautiful manifestations of Love. We can choose the path of the Magi, celebrating and gifting our true nature. Or, we can continue Herod's way, perpetuating the trauma that was enacted on us.

---

22 Firestone, *The Fantasy Bond*, 66.

On Herod's way we profoundly distrust the suggestion that the universe has our back. Herod engineers violence, death and destruction because he cannot trust that the universe is unfolding as it should. He is the prototype of a man who can never relax. He must fight for his rightful place.

In the presence of trust, love flourishes. In its absence, hatred and violence gain a foothold.

CHAPTER 12

Trust and Trustworthiness

Trust is like a vase... Once it's broken, though you can fix it, the vase will never be the same again.
— **Walter Anderson, American painter and aphorist**

The Roots of Paranoia

I feel paranoid.

Not a minute ago I was feeling deep gratitude. Many teachings were revealed in the ceremony. I was rededicating myself to the path of love, seeing clearly, feeling everything and resting in peace.

Then my mind takes a paranoid turn. I question what is happening in the ceremony. Is this a cult? What exactly is the endgame here? Is this intelligence taking over my sovereignty as an individual? What about the shaman? Maybe he's just somebody who has lost himself completely and has no choice in the matter. Who's to say that aliens haven't taken him over. If he tries to get out, maybe this intelligence punishes him so severely that he is now their slave? The chants are merely seductive attempts to remove my defenses. The fellow sitting in front of me chanting isn't working on healing me. He's breaking me. I need to escape.

Fortunately, I am not too far gone. I bring some reflection to bear on the experience. When I think about it, I remember that the shaman has shown me nothing but respect and love. His assistant is a pure-hearted man who has displayed great tenderness toward me in the ceremonies. Never once have any of them manipulated me. So what the hell is going on?

And then it hits me. Ayahuasca is known as "the Mother." As my trust deepens I start to let go of my fears. And my fear makes one last attempt to protect me. My trust issues related to my biological mother surface, only to be projected onto the medicine, the ceremony and the shaman.

Faced with this invitation to trust the Mother, the guardians of the threshold rise up to warn me. I have transgressed the limits of trust I set very early in life. My defense system goes on high alert to keep me safe. The guardians are warning me: This is how you get hurt. Turn back before it's too late!

Almost everyone who takes ayahuasca has this experience sooner or later. Broken trust breeds paranoia.

Trust is formed through a healthy attachment to the mother. A healthy attachment includes maternal affection, mirroring, appropriate and timely responses to the infant's needs related to hunger and emotional and physical comfort, and attuning to the slower rhythms of the infant. If these requirements are not met or are met inconsistently, the infant learns that intimacy is not safe.

The neuronal networks get laid down very early in life. They direct our hormonal system, when we perceive we are in danger, to prepare for a fight, take flight or freeze. You can see this freezing response in animals that have been captured by a predator. It's a sign of an immediate acceptance of their fate. When infants or young children do not receive adequate attention and affection from the mother, they receive a signal of danger — Life isn't safe! — which sets off a cascade of hormones. A tendency to act and react as though life is unsafe sets in, along with a consequent unconscious belief that "I am not safe."

The adrenal system in particular is overtaxed. The condition of hyper-vigilance, of looking out for danger, sets in early. As adults we may see danger where there is none because of this early wiring. For example, you could be sitting in a café when a stranger glances at you. You feel certain that this stranger doesn't like you. Intimacy in later life becomes challenging because under any kind of stress we can turn our lover into an enemy — all because we don't feel safe.

Fear and distrust are compounded when the infant senses that the mother (as the child ages this would include the father) needs something from him or her. My parents have their own story about the impact of their relationship on their children, as do all parents. But what I know is that when genuine intimacy and affection are absent in the parents' relationship, the children will somehow compensate.

My take is that I was set up to be a substitute for what my mother saw as an inadequate husband. She wanted me to give her what he could not: empathy, sensitivity and compassion. This was not the Freudian Oedipal complex, where the son competes with the father for the affection of the mother. I didn't want her affection. Well, of course, at one point I wanted it, but I learned that it wasn't being offered. To survive, I tuned in to her more deeply than I did to my father. I became sensitive. I saw how she rejected him and then conveyed to me, with body language, derisive comments and outright dismissal of his awkward attempts at intimacy, how inadequate he was as a husband. For too long I saw my father through my mother's eyes.

My sense of being special was not intrinsic. Rather, I was "special" because I was not like him. My specialness consisted in both seeing him as inadequate as a man and not being like him. I was adored but not loved. It wasn't me that was being adored. It was a self that contorted itself to survive.

All of this underlay my paranoia in the ceremony. I learned that the feminine was dangerous. It hated the masculine. To give in to the feminine was to be seduced into her cult of allegiance. If I wasn't vigilant I would end up as her pawn in a game whose purpose was to redeem the masculine through me. But it was too much for me. In the course of growing up I gained the nickname "golden boy." I learned how to shine but it wasn't with an inner radiance.

As an adult I had a lot of work to do to distinguish between the healthy feminine principle and my experience of my mother. I grew up with a wounded feminine. This expressed itself in a series of dreams following the ceremony. One in particular comes to mind. I'm walking in an ancient forest and come upon a cabin in the woods. There is an old blind woman with her eyes rolled back in their sockets. She is on her knees, saying prayers before bed. She is quoting from a novel. It is beautiful and elegant language. There is a bag of chamomile tea on the bed. The husband shows up. He also seems to be a wise man. I walk into the bedroom where the wife is brushing her hair. She touches my face and says, "I've seen these features before." And then, ominously, "Be careful."

A former client of mine, a fortyish woman who was sexually abused and is distrusting of men, appears and throws herself on the bed. She starts to touch my hand inappropriately, presuming an intimacy that is pure fantasy.

There are two images of the feminine in this dream: the wise crone, who is a seer (she has spiritual vision and can "see" without using her eyes); and the immature, wounded feminine, who pursues inappropriate intimacy with me. Her behavior is reminiscent of my mother's unconscious attempt to recruit me as a substitute for her husband.

The wise crone is an image for my soul (the soul is always portrayed as feminine in myth). Her inclination to memorize beautiful writing, her prayers and her choice of soothing chamomile tea are images of a healthy, trusting and even divine feminine principle. She "sees" me even though she is blind. The divine feminine has developed inner vision. Outward vision, by comparison, is blind, clouded by trauma. She looks beyond my physical features and into my soul. When she says, "I've seen this face before," it is the face of Levinas's "other," the natural, vulnerable self, that she refers to. In this she provides a corrective for my early experience of not being seen except in meeting my mother's needs. She is warning me of what is at stake if I do not allow my feminine to develop beyond the wounded feminine. I will end up as a distrusting, paranoid version of my mother.

Alice Miller's injunction to not be aware (discussed in Chapter 7) is captured in a story by G. I. Gurdjieff. He explains that a cosmic catastrophe knocked two pieces off planet Earth. These became moons, one visible, the other invisible. Given that these two moons were from the parent body of Earth, they needed to be fed. Humans served this function, energetically supplying nourishment for these two bodies. Gurdjieff says that this was the only function of humans even though they carried on as if they were free.

At some point a few humans awoke to this arrangement. As they developed what Gurdjieff calls "objective reason," their tolerance for being used to feed the moons diminished. But this awakening threatened the moon's survival. A special commission of archangels decided that the awakening must be stopped. They implanted an organ in humans, called *Kundabuffer*, the purpose of which was to confuse fantasy with reality. Ever since, only the most disciplined humans have been able to transcend the power of the *Kundabuffer*.

I have no way of knowing whether Gurdjieff took this cosmology literally. But understood as myth, the story serves us well. The invisible moon is the wounded feminine. This is the narcissistically deprived mother, whose most accessible source of nourishment is her own children. The *Kundabuffer* is both externally implanted in the form of society's sentimentalization of motherhood and the institution of the family, and internally implanted as the predisposition of the child to survive childhood. Unless the implant is removed through the painful awakening of individuation and the resultant exile from family and society, the romantic fantasy of freedom, individuality and loving connection with mother lasts a lifetime.

Is the Universe for Me, Against Me or Indifferent?

A wise teacher once told me that one of the most important things we need to sort out for ourselves on the spiritual path is whether the universe is for us, against us or indifferent.

Our beliefs on this question form unconsciously, depending on our experience of the trustworthiness of those charged with our care and nurture. As adults we default under stress to the conclusion we came to as children. When trust is broken, we form the unconscious belief and orientation that the universe is against us. We can't trust it to deliver what we need to survive, let alone thrive. We must *take* what we need. We must figure out how to get it, calculate what this other person (the mother) needs in order for us to get what we need, and then contort ourselves to fit the circumstances. Above all, we must be vigilant! What we cannot be is relaxed and spontaneous. The mantra is "It is not safe to be myself."

I spent decades unconsciously believing that the universe was against me. I organized my life and made career decisions to buffer me against a universe that could at any moment decimate me. The primary characteristic of people who hold this belief unconsciously is vigilant. They will survey the environment to determine where the danger lies and what exactly is being required of them in this circumstance. Chameleon-like, they make the necessary adjustments at lightning speed. It's fast and subtle. An on-looker would never notice. Only with careful attention can I see myself doing it.

Being in this state of red alert overwhelms the endocrine system, which regulates hormones, including adrenaline. My naturopath thought I should have my adrenal system tested. I was in overdrive and had been for decades. The tests revealed I was in stage three adrenal failure.

What is life like if you believe the universe is for you? Walking my dog, Koa, in a forest in Vancouver, I spontaneously reach down to scratch his back. I feel love for him. I can see his pleasure, which he accepts without a second thought. From his perspective, this is life. Out of nowhere, some-body reaches down and makes you feel good. If a child grows up on the receiving end of gratuitous acts of kindness, she will assume that this is what the universe does. And she will confirm that assumption every time she passes kindness on for no good reason — other than the heart of the universe, pulsing in her, is full of overflowing kindness.

Seek First the Kingdom of God

The Christian gospel, along with every other religion and new age spiritual doctrine, can be reduced to a basic message: Trust.

Jesus saw that the root of economic injustice and all manner of violence is a paranoid worldview. When there is no higher ethic than "take while the taking is good," higher values such as giving, sharing and generosity seem foolish. Most humans, unsure of their intrinsic importance, conserve their energies and store them up in the barn of a false self. In contrast, Jesus's experience was that the universe just keeps pouring itself out to pro-vide for life. His self-expression was self-emptying. He poured himself out, trusting that in so doing he was expressing the universe that was pouring itself out in generosity — like the sun, which burns six hundred million tons of hydrogen per second so that life on Earth can flourish. This is why one of his titles is "Light of the world."

Atheism and materialistic philosophy consider the sun's generosity to be a fortunate accident, not a model for life. They reduce humans to in-stinct and self-preservation in a universe that is headed for extinction. If this view is true, who can afford to be generous?

When Jesus said, "Seek first the Kingdom of God, and all these things shall be added unto you," he was addressing the issue of whether the universe or God/dess or Source is for us. Put justice, love, peace, connection with Source first. Dedicate your life to these values and then relax. (I know. That's a big ask for those of us who have trouble trusting.) In the only prayer he taught his disciples, there is a line that captures this theme well: "Give us this day our daily bread." Jesus wasn't on the Freedom 55 plan. He didn't ask what the pension plan was like before he signed on the dotted line — he expected only enough for this day, and then the next, and the next.

He warned farmers enjoying bumper crops against building bigger barns. It seems natural to us that they would want to store up some wealth as a hedge against possible drought. But, says Jesus, what good is all that stored wealth if this very night your life is demanded? The man who is rich by the standards of the world will build bigger barns. Only after they are full will he relax and "eat, drink and be merry." The woman who is rich toward God is already relaxed (Luke 12:16–21). She acts from this relaxed condition. She knows something the rest of us don't.

Jesus also warned his disciples not to worry about their bodies, what they would eat or wear. Think about ravens, he said. They don't sow or reap and have no barns to store up treasure. Yet God feeds them, and we are more valuable than ravens (Luke 12:23–24).

Putting the Kingdom first amounts to dedicating your life to spirit, and then trusting. This seems far-fetched to us in the twenty-first century. We have been steeped in a neo-Darwinian ethic that gave rise to a cutthroat and paranoid capitalism that robs us of our soul, kills the planet and steals from the poor.

Trust set Jesus free. He acted with a freedom that was absolute because he trusted that the universe (*Abba* or "daddy" in Aramaic) was for him. This depth of trust enabled him to operate from a higher motivation than safety and security. This is the basis for acting in freedom. Without trust we are not free to live a full life. All of our decisions will be in service to building a tall cedar hedge around our monitored homes, as well as building a balanced portfolio that is recession proof. We will forever test others, test God and test life to prove that our distrust is justified. We call this "being prudent."

To reclaim our freedom to be the unique and radiant beings that we are, we need to do the work of seeing how and when we closed our hearts to an abundant universe. The reason our paranoid lifestyles make sense to us is related to early attachment failures and the resultant refusal to trust.

The Tall Poppy Syndrome

The tall poppy syndrome refers to those who dare to stand out from the crowd. Tall poppies invariably act with more freedom, which correlates to trust that the universe is for them. Trust underlies the courage to be an individual. A surprising number of biblical stories address this theme. The hoi polloi who conform to social expectations often resent the freedom of the artist, poet or prophet. Think of Joseph and his coat of many colours. The special attention he received from his father set him up to stand out from the crowd. His brothers were less enthralled than their father was. They threw him in a pit, then sold him as a slave to merchants who happened to be passing by in a camel caravan. But Joseph was a man of trust. He landed on his feet in Egypt as the Pharaoh's dream interpreter. As for his brothers' betrayal, he concluded that it was the will of God. This kind of radical acceptance is born of trust that the universe is for us.

Mary had the audacity to take off her apron, leave the kitchen and join the men to hear Jesus's teaching. Her sister, Martha, resented and envied Mary, imploring Jesus to put Mary in her place. Jesus refused, saying that Mary had chosen the "better part." The better part is choosing freedom.

The elder brother in the parable of the prodigal son stayed home while the younger brother ventured out to see the world, make his mistakes and return home his own person. The elder brother hated him for acting in freedom. Then, to add further insult, the father threw a party for the prodigal!

Religious authorities couldn't tolerate Jesus's originality. His freedom to act and teach outside the boundaries of convention inspired envy. He lived moment by moment according to the idiosyncratic spiritual guidance he was receiving, rather than by religious or political ideology. Judas initiated the violence against Jesus that would end in Jesus's death because Jesus wouldn't buy into his Zealot ideology, or any other ideology.

Underlying the unusual degree of freedom enjoyed by all tall poppies is trust. They transcend convention and yet are still provided for in a world that rewards playing it safe. Even if these individuals die poor and wretched, as many artists and prophets do, they would never dream of exchanging their freedom for security. Philosopher and critic Colin Wilson calls these courageous souls the "outsiders." They gall conventional society. Historically, our species is not kind to these souls. Any person who displays more freedom, more individuality and more spontaneity than average risks ridicule, shame or even death.

In a session with my therapist, on LSD, I morph into an eight-month-old. I'm not walking yet. I crawl toward him and make eye contact. Then I crawl to the other side of the room and look back to see if he is still there. I repeat this for thirty minutes or more. I am reprogramming myself, discovering that his presence is constant even if I venture off. I am teaching myself that the universe has my back. I can feel my brain and nervous system becoming rewired. This venturing out, checking in, venturing further is the toddler's way of discovering that his impulse for greater freedom will be supported.

This is just a start, however. It takes a lot of practice to rewire the nervous system. I developed a series of eight Core Agreements for being human in community. One of these is *Fail Bravely.* Great men and women try and fail, often dozens of times, before succeeding. J.K. Rowling received several rejection letters from publishers after submitting *Harry Potter and the Philosopher's Stone.* Even after the Harry Potter series became a worldwide bestseller, her later novels, submitted under a pseudonym, were rejected by publishers. One of the kinder responses, from Constable and Robinson Publishing House, suggested that she take a writing course. They also gave her tips about how to submit a book proposal. The rejection letter ended with: "I regret that we have reluctantly come to the conclusion that we could not publish it with commercial success."

When we put ourselves out there and discover that we can survive rejection — that is, we don't interpret rejection as yet another occasion of the universe being against us — we teach our brain and nervous system that taking risks and failing is not the end of the world or the end of us. Even though rejection *was* the end of our world when we were too young to understand why we were shamed or punished when we tried something new.

Courage

After trust has been broken, and after we've done all the trauma work, we still need to summon courage. Courage is the discipline of seeing life for what it is, including suffering and misery and yet "praising in spite of," to use Colin Wilson's phrase. It is the recognition of the mystic and prophet that life is not only suffering and misery. They see the glorious transcendent dimension within this earthly sphere.

Ordinary consciousness, says Wilson, is a liar. The problem with the French existentialists, he offers, is that they refused to exercise the full range of consciousness, which includes the "absurd good news" that life is an inestimable gift and that we are fortunate to be here to experience it.

I refer the reader to my experience of the wheat field in the autumn sun after reading a simple line of poetry (see Chapter 9). The ecstasy I experienced is the *real* world. W. B. Yeats captures this sense of "absurd good news" in his poem "Vacillation":

> *My fiftieth year had come and gone,*
> *I sat, a solitary man,*
> *In a crowded London shop,*
> *An open book and empty cup*
> *On the marble table-top.*
> *While on the shop and street I gazed*
> *My body of a sudden blazed;*
> *And twenty minutes more or less*
> *It seemed, so great my happiness,*
> *That I was blessed and could bless.*

This is the poetry of a "solitary man." He has broken free of the collective consciousness and discovered for himself an overflow of meaning in ordinary life.

Early in my recovery with ayahuasca and psychedelics I had a dream. A physician is prescribing a pill that I need to take. It is called "seclusion." The pill is enormous and very difficult to swallow.

At the time of the dream, after twenty-eight years of a very public and demanding career, my previous five years had been spent apart from the world. This was not easy. Indeed, it had been difficult to swallow. I was reminded of those cop films where the hero orders the villain to "Step away from the car." Only I was being commanded to "Step away from your life." A time of solitude seems to be the only way to get enough perspective to realize that we've been living a partial life.

The kind of experience Yeats writes about in this poem rarely comes to those who have not become world-weary, causing them to withdraw from the superficiality and triviality of everyday life. This world negation is not the end, however. It may give rise to a new sense of world affirmation. Only after this period of seclusion are we able to see the "Life we have lost in living" (T. S. Eliot, *Choruses from the Rock*).

The challenge, says Wilson, is to discipline our minds so we are able to call up this state of expanded consciousness at will. It is cowardly and lazy, he says, to succumb to despair and gloom. More than this, it is an evasion of our responsibility to become visionaries of what is possible.

When we succumb to despair, it is a signal that we are gripped by a memory of failed attachment. This memory threatens to overwhelm and supersede our imaginative faculty, that aspect of consciousness that Yeats experienced in the London coffee shop. In effect, we are regressing to the early experience of misery and sorrow in the hope that surely somebody this time will rescue us. But there is nobody coming. All we have left to do is grieve. This too requires courage, particularly for men, who have been socialized toward stoic denial of feelings. Men have confused unwillingness to feel with heroism. After the grief we must seize life actively and refuse to believe the helplessness and powerlessness.

The true hero is the mystic and the prophet who trusts that, despite everything, it's all "rigged in our favour" (Rumi). Neither the suffering of others nor our own trauma justifies a loss of trust that the universe is for us. The heroes of our age imagine what Charles Eisenstein calls "the better world our hearts know is possible," and then rally their energies towards its realization. They do not let bitterness, cynicism or pessimism steer the ship of their soul.

When Nelson Mandela was unjustly imprisoned for twenty-seven years in South Africa, he frequently recited the poem "Invictus" to his fellow inmates. His soul was indomitable. This poem, written by Ernest William Henley in 1875, captures the courage of the visionary hero that Wilson champions. His trust in a universe that is for him never wavers.

Out of the night that covers me,
Black as the pit from pole to pole,
I thank whatever gods may be
for my unconquerable soul.
In the fell clutch of circumstance
I have not winced nor cried aloud.
Under the bludgeonings of chance
My head is bloody, but unbowed.
Beyond this place of wrath and tears
Looms but the Horror of the shade,
And yet the menace of the years
Finds and shall find me unafraid.
It matters not how strait the gate,
How charged with punishments the scroll,
I am the master of my fate:
I am the captain of my soul.

Trusting Enough to Go for Love

For years I prayed that I would find a woman I could love with all my heart. I stayed in my previous marriage for all the wrong reasons: family, financial security, career. As well, I didn't want to cause suffering. My timidity broke the aforementioned cardinal rule of my wise therapist: "Endure nobody and nothing."

One day my prayer was answered. The knowing was immediate. I was thrown into a crisis. The universe was calling my bluff. "Okay, dude, if you are serious, here you go." I remember the day I found out that she, too, had been waiting for me. When she told me, I walked away with two words sounding in my head: "I'm fucked." I would need to end a twenty-eight-year marriage. My finances would be decimated. My career would be over because the congregation I had been serving could not roll with this. I had friends who would never speak to me again. Was I willing to step off the cliff for the sake of love? Would I have the courage to start over from scratch? I knew that I couldn't live with myself if I refused the gift. It would represent a conscious denial of Spirit in my mind. And if I did go for it, I would be fucked because life as I knew it would be over.

I stepped off the cliff. But if you think this meant my troubles were over, you'd be wrong. As they say, "Wherever you go, there you are." I brought my unresolved trauma with me into this new relationship.

Every single one of my trust issues reared its ugly head not long after the relationship began. In fact, these issues came up more strongly with this new woman than ever before. This is because she refused to tiptoe around my unresolved trauma. She challenged me to grow. In the beginning I didn't see it as a loving challenge. I saw a power trip. I saw control. Yep, you guessed it. I saw my mother through the eyes of a three-year-old. When she confronted me, I went into hysterical opposition. When we fought, I couldn't stay connected. A huge "fuck you" surfaced that didn't belong to her. (Okay, sometimes it did.) When we were in conflict, I assumed that she had all the power and I was helpless. I truly did not trust that she was for me or had my best interests at heart. I was convinced, when things got difficult, that she was out to get me. It's embarrassing to admit this. But intimate relationship is where we got wounded, and intimate relationship is where the healing gold is found.

There is one more dimension of trust that bears mentioning. Those who trust that the universe is for them are more nomadic by nature. They are less attached to having their life follow a particular form and are willing to trust an internal impulse to pull up stakes. My experience of the ayahuasca and psychedelic community bears this out. A great many of these pilgrims have left the security of conventional jobs and lifestyles to follow the Spirit.

There is a story in the Old Testament depicting an era when there was a serious debate about building God a temple. After all, the surrounding cultures all had houses for their God. The temple epitomized security and power in the world. But those people who followed another mystic tradition thought this was sacrilege. Their ancestors had travelled about the wilderness as nomads, trusting in a God who would not be domesticated.

Who Told You I Need a House?
"Who told you I need a house?"
asks the nomad G_d
of those who grew weary of the eternal restlessness,

thinking S/He might appreciate
a fixed address
like a Queen or a priest.

"Your temples
conceal streams of grace
where once desert pilgrims
found respite, quenched thirst, offered thanks
and then felt the mistrals moving them on.

Manager priests in fixed and fancy offices
do not feel the wind
or hear the gurgling music.

Am I being too harsh?
Look into your eyes.
A creation story explodes when,
in every astonished moment,
you behold
the adventure of life
as my advent.
Look again. Steady.
I am in that retinal explosion —
in the still, black centre,
and in the lines of light that converge
in the you of this moment,
and extend from the you of this moment
outward to encompass a future
that is born of my restlessness.

Bang!

If you must build your houses,
then make them sacraments of Sophia —
more mobile than motion.

Tilt the foundation
toward the future,
so that in short order
gravity pours even the most
reluctant inhabitants
out the open door
to join the procession of pilgrims,
led by the one who has no place
to rest his head.

Yes, I am unrelenting.
But you knew this.
Your bright and searching eyes always knew it,
before the dullness of the Great Domestication set in.
I do want more.
It's that simple.
You may think this cruel
if you have already fallen in love
with the form of your life.

But even your houses of love
will be shattered and swept away
by the tide of Love itself — and without apology —
to become an anthropologist's artifact,
an interesting study of how an earlier love
was constructed.
I want to transcend myself
in you.

Befriend fear,
that unsolicited angel
appearing at the tent
of your life,
come to announce
that the Wild One
is breaking camp and moving on.

Time to pull up stakes.
Again.
Nobody (not the Nazarene for sure)
said it would be easy.
Here's my one concession
to your fear:

Lean back.
I will carry you for a time
in the momentum of my yearning.
The Future asks — only —
for your trust."

But Am I Trustworthy?

In the ceremony, after getting to the bottom of my trust issues, a question explodes within me: *What about you, Bruce? Are you trustworthy? Why should anybody trust you? Are you good with your word?*

Shit! It's one thing to see the ways that I've been betrayed. It's another to look at my betrayals of others. All my broken promises parade before my eyes. Every covenant I broke surfaces. Thus ensues another epic purge. I need to feel the hurt I caused and then be cleansed of all the accumulated grief and guilt.

Before the ceremony I hadn't given this a second thought. But this is what happens on the medicine. Your soul gets the opportunity to set a new standard for what it means to be truly human instead of your adapted, survivor self.

We let ourselves off the hook too easily. When I step back and look at my life from the perspective of Spirit, I wonder if I am trustworthy.

"Woe is me," lamented the prophet Isaiah when he was taken up to the throne of the holy. "I am a man of unclean lips."

He saw his impurity relative to all that is sacred. It's not through the eyes of withering judgment that we see ourselves clearly, though, but through eyes of compassion. We see how lost we've been, and how we've been living without a guiding star.

In the sharing circle the next day I blurt out, "Don't trust me. I am not trustworthy."

The shaman tries to soften my proclamation by pointing out all the ways he does indeed trust me. And so I clarify. When I am acting unconsciously — which is the traumatized self — I am not connected to and trusting in Source. Therefore, I am not to be trusted.

It's an on–off proposition. We're either in survivor mode or in Source mode. If I'm in survivor mode, I'm not trustworthy because everything I do will be about me and my survival. I will treat the people I meet as Its, holding them as a means to my survivalist ends, and not as Thous (Martin Buber). Every decision will be in the service of survival.

I realize that this sounds absolutist. But I have learned on the medicine that there actually are some absolutes. This offends our postmodernist sensibility, which holds that your truth is as good as my truth which is as good as any truth. But the difference between the absolutes I experience on the medicine and those set down by fundamentalist religions or politics is that mine aren't based in any belief system or ideology. I'm not being shown anybody else's way, just my own. This is what happens when I plug into Source. There is an uncompromising beckoning to be ever more human.

After the ceremony my shaman asks if I would transport the precious medicine back to Vancouver for him. It is the perfect gesture for a man questioning his trustworthiness. This is how the medicine works. I don't know if my shaman is aware of it or not. But I take it as a sign that the universe is showing me I am indeed trustworthy — at least to do this much.

In the next chapter I share an intuition, based on my experience in the medicine, that the universe or Source or God/dess is actively on the lookout for trustworthy souls. We are being recruited for love, by love.

CHAPTER 13

Recruited

How should the soul not take wings
when from the Glory of God
It hears a sweet kindly call:
"Why are you here, soul? Arise!"

— **Rumi**

Recruited for Love

Early in an LSD session with my therapist I look at him and say, "You get it, don't you? There aren't many who get it, but I can see you get it."

What I have tapped into is the realization that he answered the call of love and gave himself over. He is one who said yes to that call, whatever the cost. And the cost is everything that is not love. It is suffering the letting go of most of what the world has to offer. In the moment I feel like we are part of a secret society scattered across the planet whose members know what their lives are for. It isn't a cult. There are no membership rites. It's just a quiet, felt recognition that some are all in and some are not, but all are called.

The universe is in the recruiting business. We are being recruited for love. That's what is revealed to me when I am in the medicine. This recruitment is not conscription, which is involuntary. And it is not proselytizing, which is imposing an ideology or belief system. Jesus recruited. But he wasn't recruiting to start a new church or a new religion. And it wasn't about believing in anything, especially him. His recruitment was a response to a direct experience that love is at the centre of this evolutionary process, and love is alluring us toward a completion — the completion being the incarnation of the True Human.

His birth, life, death and resurrection make up the story of the realization of the New Human. It is one attempt to show what the universe is doing, what it is aimed at. His life is a glimpse of what is possible for all of us. He lay down the evolutionary groove for the rest of us. The gospels are a vision of where we're heading as a species. A serious reader can't help but find within their pages a beckoning to become, an invitation to make one's life a sincere step toward a completion of our species. When I'm honest and truly listening, not just to this ancient text but to my own life, this summons is constant. But mostly we're not listening. We're distracted.

Evil

The radical corollary is that if we refuse this summons to dedicate ourselves to love, we leave the door open to what is not love. We must use our freedom to choose which path we're on. Evil is the enactment of hatred and violence. When I'm on the medicine, a traditional worldview that recognizes the reality of evil comes online: It comes with a strong sense that evil is an active force in the world, with an agenda to subvert the evolution of our species. I know this sounds regressive to modern ears — like I'm some kind of fundamentalist. But I'm not. I have no interest in institutional religion or in perpetuating any kind of dogma.

In the ceremony, when I see how my perpetrators hurt me, I say to them, "You agreed to evil." Again, it is an on–off proposition. If we are not choosing love we are ceding the territory to evil, hatred and violence. We are also seeding those who are on the receiving end of our violence with evil. I see, in the medicine, how unkindness, the refusal to be tender, the acting out of rage opened me up as a toddler to evil.

Where there is no love, a void opens up in our body and energy field where love is meant to be. And as shamans have known for millennia, this void is an opening, an entrance, for malevolent energies that don't actually belong.

In all my years as a clergyman I didn't take evil seriously. I was "progressive," a modernist. Evil could be explained away as an evolutionary hangover from our reptilian and mammalian ancestry that was built right into our brain stem. It was biologically based. But my experience on the medicine tells a different story. I saw and felt malevolent energetic presences looking for opportunities.

However, the reality of evil doesn't mean we can escape responsibility for our actions. Flip Wilson did a famous comedy routine with the punch line "The devil made me do it." That's never true. As adults, even when we're in the grips of unconscious trauma, we do not lose the capacity to choose. Every act of hatred and violence is a choice.

St. Paul concluded that there was a law of the flesh and a law of the Spirit. The closer we get to living by the law of the Spirit in a dedicated way, the more the law of the flesh arises to lure us back to a baser existence. This dynamic opposition to the way of love does not arise if we have never truly committed ourselves to this path. If we hang out on neutral ground, remaining unconscious of our higher calling, we do not threaten the forces of darkness. But the moment we get serious, the spiritual battle is on. Then we are tested. And then our eyes open to what is at stake.

Herod, *The Matrix* and Big Pharma

The story of the Magi coming to witness the birth of the Christ child again comes to mind. They saw in the stars that one was born to lead the world away from violence and hatred, and toward peace. Herod was the representative of Rome in the region where Jesus was born. The Empire only knew one way, the Pax Romana, which was peace through violent domination. Jesus would teach peace through justice and love.

Herod desired an audience with the Magi. He wished to find out where the Christ child had been born — so he could destroy him. But the Magi were not innocents. They knew the evil in his heart and in the heart of Empire. They returned home "a different way" so Herod could not capture them. And then, as the story goes, the slaughter began. Herod ordered the murder of all Jewish children under the age of two to ensure that love could not disrupt the kingdom of this world.

This is not history. The New Testament holocaust never happened. And yet, as with all good myth, it is always happening. The history of holocausts reveals the darkness that is always just a choice away. George Lucas has made a fortune off his depiction of the battle between good and evil. *Star Wars* is one of the highest-grossing series of films ever made. At the core is the story of the battle between Darth Vader and the Jedi. Darth Vader was once a Jedi but chose the dark side; his son, Luke Skywalker, chose the light. *Star Wars* is an old myth told in a contemporary medium. Each new movie in the series captures the imagination of the public with its portrayal of the battle between good and evil.

Or think of the trilogy *The Matrix.* The humans don't realize that their lives are a computer-generated algorithm. They proceed with the illusion of freedom although their life is programmed. They are humans, but because they are asleep they might as well be robots. Now and then one of them intuits that something is off, that they are not really living a true life. When Neil has intimations of this, the resistance, led by Morpheus and Trinity, enters the computer program to offer him an opportunity to escape the program. He is being recruited. The existential crisis and opportunity he faces is whether he will accept that he is "the one" charged to lead the revolution against the Matrix.

Neil is offered two pills, a red one and a blue one. The decision to use pills to symbolize the moment of choice is interesting. Take the red one and you will awaken and join the resistance. Take the blue one and go back to your programmed life. There are references in the Matrix to psychedelic substances such as mescaline. I wonder whether Lana and Lilly Wachowski, who wrote and directed the movies, were suggesting that the red pill represented the promise of psychedelics to wake us up so we could join the resistance and the path of love, even though it would entail suffering, sacrifice and leaving the realm of what we imagined reality to be. In contrast, the blue pill represents Big Pharma's solution to our suffering — pills that treat the symptoms but not the underlying trauma. They soothe the suffering but leave the user trapped in the Matrix of convention.

In time, Neil accepts that he is "the one." He is given a new name, Neo, that suggests a new kind of human and reflects his spiritual identity as one charged with liberating humanity, starting with himself. Neo, of course, is each one of us, recruited by love to exit the world of illusion, entrapment and false security — to awaken, that is, to the truth that each of us is being recruited to be "the one."

One character, Zypher, is the Judas figure in the story. He betrays the resistance and returns to the Matrix. Zypher says, "After nine years you know what I realize? Ignorance is bliss." This is always an option, a temptation to the regressive alternative. He would rather be happy in the illusion than endure the hardships and rewards of freedom.

But when we make that choice, we are being recruited by evil, the darkness of unconsciousness, and by the depersonalized system that is invested in keeping us passive and obedient citizens.

This is illustrated vividly by Aldous Huxley in his novel *Brave New World,* which depicts a world where Big Pharma has perfected a pleasure drug, soma, that keeps people happy. Soma offers "all the advantages of Christianity and alcohol, but without any of the side effects." It allows everyone to fuse into a common identity and the feeling that "we are all one." The protagonist, Bernard, is suspicious of the euphoric narcotic and resists the call of the so-called Greater Being that takes away individuality and personhood and turns everyone into obedient servants of the system. Huxley, like Levinas, sees the dangers of sacrificing individuality to the prevailing ideology of the state, church or family system.

Conscious Evolution

The challenge for humans is that, like other animals, we develop automatically up to a certain age. Our motor skills, strength, intelligence, perspective and creativity develop without our conscious participation. Until the question of the meaning of life struck me in my second year of undergraduate studies, I was not bothered by my development. Sports, girls and partying were sufficient pursuits. The true mystery is why, and whence, this question of meaning even arose. Unexpectedly, I was being summoned to a new level of existence. My aforementioned pastimes were rendered insufficient, contextualized by…what? And then an evangelist presented me with an explicit summons from one of the greatest and most influential figures of history. Why was I even interested?

Pierre Teilhard de Chardin interprets the evolutionary imperative as a summons from *bien être* to *plus être,* from well-being to *more* being. His theology, though brilliant, is less important than his intuition that within the evolutionary process itself there is an allurement to more. George Bernard Shaw's Secondborn, in the play *Buoyant Billions,* realizes "I don't want to be happy; I want to be alive and active." When we lose touch with this internal drive for the more, or turn our backs on it, we experience life failure.

This evolutionary impulse works in us unconsciously and carries us passively up to a certain age, when we either activate our will and begin consciously participating in our own evolution or we stop developing. Colin Wilson's study of outsiders in history shows that these people, often artists, writers, poets, dancers and novelists, took up the evolutionary challenge and summons to become "more." But, like most of us, they fall short of full self-realization. They are critical of how the human race has fallen short of its potential. The superficiality and triviality of the world they see disgusts them, and they may start to loathe themselves for not being able to transcend it. This is what sets them outside conventional culture, a separation compounded by there being very few people who can understand what they are experiencing. Most seem happy enough with the way things are. And if they are not happy, it does not occur to them that there is anything to be done.

Dying into Life

I recall, early in my career as a minister, being enraptured by Ernest Becker's Pulitzer Prize-winning book *The Denial of Death,* an extended meditation on the way in which the fear of death is the motivating force behind civilizations and monuments, wars and personality formation. No doubt Becker has a point. His conclusion, however, is based on the belief that the reality of death leaves us with an unresolvable dilemma. Yet I myself have experienced an acute awareness of mortality following an experience of love and joy. My response was a bittersweet sadness. It was a wake-up call — the gift of death — not to fritter away my life. I began to feel like Becker's grand scheme was a denial of *life*.

In the medicine I have been summoned to die on more than one occasion. In my time on the mountain I dreamed that a huge nursing log, a fallen majestic Douglas fir, suddenly stood straight up. Towering above me, she summoned me to come to her. I walked toward her and became entangled in her roots, then disintegrated into her body. She gently lay me back down on the forest floor.

The meaning was instantly clear to me. I saw that a nursing log is not dead. A tree's spirit doesn't die. Its decomposition is nothing other than a stage of life. Though it is true that this particular tree will never stand again, except in my dreams, it will live forever in the life it is nourishing by dying. The nursing log was teaching me how to die before death so that I might become sustenance for future lives. Surely this is what it means to become an elder.

It's only when we are attached to our small egos that death seems ultimate and in opposition to life. We identify so closely with our current personality structure that we set up death as the enemy and bogyman. When we refuse to face death, it looms larger than life. The idea then prevails that death makes a mockery of life. But, in fact, death is in service of life.

In another dream I arrive at a party. The table is set for all the guests, with placemats and designated seats. I excitedly look for my name — and find it at the top of every placemat: "In Memoriam: The Life of Bruce Sanguin." I am at my own funeral!

Becker is right from one point of view. If we cannot face death, it becomes our master. Avoiding death becomes our chief motivation. When we can neither avoid it nor face it, we become morbid and depressed. We may feel as though there is nothing to be done. It looms larger than life, rendering further living pointless. It becomes our god.

The god of death has demanded the premature sacrifice of too many artists and poets, who go further than most of us in unflinchingly facing it. Thomas Lovell Beddoes was one such poet and dramatist. He took poison, ending his life at forty-five. Early in life he entered medicine with the hope of discovering physical evidence that the spirit survives death. He was a man drawn to "more being," but was unsuccessful in finding it. He became obsessed by death. In his play *Death's Jest Book*, the Duke delivers the following morbid speech:

> *The look of the world's a lie,*
> *a face made up o'er graves and fiery depths,*

and nothing's true but what is horrible.
If man could see the perils and diseases he elbows
Each day he walks a mile,
which catch at him, which fall behind
and graze him as he passes,
Then would he know that life's a single pilgrim
Fighting unarmed among a thousand soldiers.

What is lacking is a powerful enough experience of what Jesus called "abundant life" in John's gospel.

A font of creativity, vitality and love gave birth to this universe. It left, and continues to leave, expressions of itself scattered throughout an ever-expanding universe. This abundance is where my dream of the Douglas fir came from, showing me that there is nothing to be afraid of and that the purpose of my life is laying it down so that others may share in the abundance. This abundance is also the source of the undying search in me for love, and my intolerance of all that is not love. When we take that mystery as what is most real and true and identify with it — meaning *I Am That* in human form — we tap into an eternal well of vitality, meaning and purpose. From this place a "Yes" to the invitation of life arises naturally and spontaneously.

CHAPTER 14

The Practice

At the end of an ayahuasca journey, I was given four life practices. I suppose you could call them spiritual practices, but "spiritual" somehow feels divorced from life. These were down-to-earth, like instructions for how to proceed in life. I've said it before, but it bears repeating: The work of integrating our medicine journeys into the way we live our life is the whole point of the exercise. When this doesn't happen, people can get hooked on the "big experience," returning to the medicine again and again, without seeing much significant change in their lives.

It's not like I heard voices telling me these were the practices I was to follow. They didn't come to me in linear time but as an all-at-once knowing, what the mystics called "gnosis." Historically, this direct knowing freaked the church out. If this kind of knowing caught on, the church hierarchy feared there might soon be no need for priests or the Bible.

So here are my four life practices that I received in the ceremony:

1. Bow (Cultivate reverence, devotion, and gratitude).
2. Show impeccable hospitality (Treat everyone who comes into your teepee as the princes and princesses that they are).
3. Move at the pace of life (No faster, no slower).
4. Leave the rest to me.

I. Bow

The Journey to My Knees

I've taken 150 micrograms of LSD, a relatively small dose. I'm lying on a divan waiting for the effects to kick in. After an hour I turn toward an altar beside the sofa. On it is a candelabrum with four orange candles. A spray of red fireweed peeks over the lip of a small vase. Completing the arrangement is a braid of sweetgrass that I used to purify myself and the space, another red candle in the shape of a rose, two acorns and some small crystals. The late afternoon light is shining through the window, illuminating this scene.

The more I focus on the light, the more it glows, until it is not the sun's light but another source of light that is illuminating everything from within. Mystics call this the *uncreated* light. I always wondered what this would look like. There is a luminescent cobweb with many small diamond-like nodes, all shining with different colours. I am seeing perfection, harmony and exquisite beauty. I had asked to know Source directly, and for me, this was an answer to that prayer.

The delicacy of it causes me to feel fragile. I crawl off the divan to my knees and place my forehead on the ground in a gesture of devotion and gratitude. I see in this moment that spiritual practice is nothing more or less than resonating with the frequency of Source energy, matching my frequency with the frequency of Source. The way to achieve this is through a posture of devotion. I am in alignment with the frequency of the light. Words are unnecessary.

I see how my ego resists this devotional state. On my knees in prayerful devotion, the ego dissolves. It just isn't present. Rather, "I" am not present. The construction I know as "Bruce" is gone. It cannot be expressed in words. I see myself and everything in creation as incarnations of that exquisite harmony, beauty and light. I know that I won't find peace until I allow myself to resonate at this delicate frequency — and let it be "me." There won't be peace in my life, or peace in the world, without matching this frequency from within.

Time slows down, way down. I am being shown the slowest possible measure of time, until I exit time altogether into timelessness. Then silence.

This silence is more than the absence of sound. It is a presence. Eternity doesn't mean living forever. It means the end of time altogether.

The "Fear of the Lord" Is Not What You're Thinking

Another ceremony. The ayahuasca tea brings me to my knees through awe. Ayahuasca appears to me as a serpent with colourful feathers. As the medicine comes on, this serpent moves very slowly and majestically through my entire body. While the serpent moves through my body, my job is to show profound respect and to hold very still.

When this vision appeared to me, I understood what the Jewish scriptures meant by "fear of the Lord." *Yirah* is the Hebrew word for fear, and yes, it can mean fear of punishment (by the God who hates evil). But its highest meaning is more like awe or reverence.

> *And now, Israel, what does the Lord require of you, but to fear (yirah) the Lord, your God, to walk in all his ways, to love him and serve him with all your heart and soul. (Deuteronomy 10:12)*

Awe and reverence are the necessary predispositions to walk the path, to love and be in service. It was awe and reverence I felt as this super-intelligent being appeared in my vision and passed slowly through my body. One wisdom teaching states that the "fear of the Lord is the beginning of wisdom" (Proverbs 19:23). Wisdom is not knowing facts. It's knowing how to live. Awe and reverence are the starting point for how to live.

Gordon Wasson, a New York banker-turned-mycologist, discovered awe after taking magic mushrooms with a Mexican curandera, Maria Sabina, in 1955. His experience with psilocybin led him to write: "Ecstasy! In common parlance ecstasy is fun...But ecstasy is not fun. Your soul is seized and shaken until it tingles. After all, who will choose to feel undiluted awe...The unknowing, vulgar abuse of the word; we must recapture its full and terrifying sense."

There was a time in the evolution of humans when life itself was viewed with undiluted awe. All of life was ceremonialized in recognition that, through life, the Great Mystery was made visible and knowable.

The seasonal cycles, the waxing and waning of the moon, the planting of seeds, harvest, the movement of the herd, the hunt and the kill, birth and death, the teaching of children — all were awe-inspiring mysteries, marked by ceremony. The world was alive with presence. Even the four directions are experienced as living beings when the world is known this way.

But those days are gone. Modern materialist beliefs divide our living from sacred ceremony. You'd be considered a kook if you lit sweetgrass or offered tobacco at the start of your workday, giving thanks and asking that your industry might be in the service of the Great Spirit and humanity. We reserve one hour a week, if at all, for "religion."

"Forfeit awe, and the world becomes your marketplace," says Hebrew mystic, theologian and philosopher Abraham Heschel. Awe is the capacity to let the other be the other without having to appropriate and incorporate it into the ego.

In Dostoyevsky's *The Brothers Karamazov,* one of the brothers, Alyosha, awakens from a dream after a period of profound discouragement. He is overwhelmed with "universal consciousness." The stars speak to him: "There seemed to be threads from all those innumerable worlds of God, linking his soul to them…It was as though some idea had seized the sovereignty of his mind." Alyosha falls to the earth, weeping: "He could not have told why he longed…to kiss it…[and] to love it for ever and ever."

Mystical experiences are brief moments when, as William Blake wrote, the doors of perception are cleansed. The world hasn't changed; we have. These experiences awaken us to love — to love everything and everybody. The "universal consciousness" Dostoyevsky describes is an expanded consciousness that goes beyond, but includes our habituated way of perceiving. In this state, we realize that true freedom is only possible when we can break free from the prison of this habituated perspective. Before these experiences, nobody could have convinced us that we were imprisoned. Or more accurately, that we are the prison we are living in!

In *The Brothers Karamazov,* Father Zossima speaks from this kind of perceptual shift. He sees that we are called to love everything: "Brothers, have no fear of men's sin. Love a man even in his sin, for that is the semblance of Divine Love and is the highest love on earth. Love all God's creation, the whole and every grain of sand in it. Love every leaf, every ray of God's light. Love the animals, love the plants, love everything. If you love everything, you will perceive the divine mystery in things. Once you perceive it, you will begin to comprehend it better every day. And you will come at last to love the whole world with an all-embracing love."

How Quickly We Forget

These experiences are not as rare as we might think. I was once asked to write down ten spiritual experiences that evoked awe, then ceremonially give thanks for them while placing them in a fire. I was skeptical that I could come up with ten. I was wrong. My life had been showered with such experiences.

What disturbed me was how quickly I forgot. In my forgetfulness, I default to a belief that this flatland existence is the *real* world. This is a core dilemma of humans in the twenty-first century. Why don't we value these peak experiences to such an extent that we affirm *they* represent the real world? Many of us succumb to despair because we treat peak experiences as if they were the result of our consciousness playing tricks on us.

At some point, we need to choose. Will we trust that reality is what comes into view in these states of expanded consciousness — which causes us, like Alyosha, to fall to the ground and "love it for ever and ever"? Or will we cling tenaciously to the world created by a survivor consciousness? If we choose the former, we will do everything in our power to "cleanse the doors of perception."

Brain research may have found a correlation between these two different modes of consciousness and our bicameral brains. The left brain is metaphorically occupied by the scientist and the rationalist. It mediates the unity of reality by breaking it down into components, abstracting them from the unity, and conceptualizing everything. This makes possible great scientific advances that have served humans well. The right brain is occupied by the poet and the mystic. It mediates the unity of reality by seeing the gestalt, or the whole. It sees the patterns. But it also sees whatever we're looking at before the left brain has given it a name. We see the uniqueness and particularity of a thing before we domesticate it and become habituated to it. In the last few hundred years, we have privileged the left-brain scientist to such a degree that the right brain's poetic and artistic faculties have atrophied. Psychedelics reverse this, privileging the right-brain way of mediating reality. Both sides are necessary, but if we are dominated by the left brain, we will experience less awe.

Colin Wilson, concludes that if we live for enough years locked into left-brain consciousness, the "robot" takes over. The robot is useful. It enables us to, for example, drive a car on automatic pilot while making plans for a holiday. I am able to type these pages without having to command my fingers. But it also can take over functions that are meant to be sacred, such as making love to my wife. The robot, in modernity, has taken the reins to such an extent that life seems dull and drab. The trick, says Wilson, is to take back control from the robot, so that he is once again serving us. When the robot is in control, nothing is new. Life becomes automated. Or, rather, we become the robot, which causes us to see life as drab.

A depressed person looks out at the world and sees only a gray, dull affair. It is, he is convinced, the world as it is. Life becomes one damned thing after another. He feels that there is nothing to be done about it. But another person, who has control of his inner robot, sees a world of beauty, endless opportunity, synchronistic occurrences that make life meaningful. He lives with gratitude and with a sense that every day is a new day. To be honest, both these people live within me. Life is a continual challenge to say "no" to the robot and "yes" to the mystic way of seeing.

Ordinary consciousness is a liar, says Wilson. It's the robot colonizing us, hypnotizing us into a deluded state of passivity. It causes us to believe that the tip of the iceberg is reality. But underneath there is a massive region of consciousness where myth, poetry, art, dreams, the collective unconscious and the memory of our entire evolutionary history lives. It is in this massive region, outside the dimension of time as we know it, that we will find our vitality, enthusiasm, positivity and meaning. These, in turn, give rise to awe and reverence. The waking ego's job is to connect to and direct this massive energy source. Until we get the robot out of the driver's seat, the religious feelings that naturally arise in response to this font of creative energy are squelched.

This vast region of the subconscious, including the direct experience of Spirit, is what we are given access to on the medicine.

The task is to concentrate in a disciplined manner until the world as it is — a world of beauty and meaning — reveals itself. This is the realm of devotional consciousness, the only sane response to this life of mystery.

Gratitude

After the serpent moves through my body in the ceremony, I am directed to put my hands together in the prayer position, place my thumbs on my forehead and bow toward the heart. Try it. Hold this position for thirty seconds or more. You may discover one or more of the following things happen: less thinking; no thinking at all; deeper, more rhythmic breathing; a sense of calm; absence of worry; feelings of gratitude.

When I was twelve years old, I remember walking home from school at noon hour. I was lost in reverie, feeling lucky that I got a chance to be. I thought about all those who didn't get the same chance at life: to breathe, play basketball, race maple keys in the spring runoff by the curbside, smell the pavement after rain on a scorching summer day. It was my first experience of gratitude, the first time I can remember thinking that I might never have been, and that my existence was a matter of sheer good luck that had nothing to do with me. There was a bigger mystery at work. I wouldn't have called it God or grace or anything so highfalutin as that. I was just grateful for whatever got me here.

I think that's what the serpent was trying to get across to me. But I had to unlearn a whole lot of shit, and do a lot of puking, before my ego would get anywhere near my knees or would allow me to be caught with hands together, praying over my heart. I know that sounds strange for a clergyman. But remember, I belonged to a denomination that has serious debates about allowing an atheist to lead a congregation.

Somewhere along the road of growing up I lost the easy gratitude of that twelve-year-old. In Chapter 8, on forgiveness, I suggested that when we've been emotionally wounded, we might form a belief that life owes us something. We've been taken from, against our will, and life bloody well had better make up for it. The way back to gratitude I proposed is to suffer the heartbreak consciously and get on with life.

Frequently in ayahuasca ceremonies I've had the experience that everything is pure gift. It's almost like I don't have gratitude. It has me. It possesses me, and I become it. My separate self falls away and the words come pouring out of my mouth, "Thank you, thank you, thank you." I never feel more human or more alive that when I feel gratitude.

The illusion of insufficiency, which is the hallmark of the ego, dissolves. The universe is rushing toward you with everything you need. More than this, you understand that you are the fruit of this evolutionary tree. I saw myself as a necessary and valuable outgrowth of a single, evolutionary process. I saw that I belonged.

2. Show Impeccable Hospitality

The second practice was impeccable hospitality. The instructions were "Treat everyone who comes into your teepee as the princes and princesses that they are." Which is strange. I'm not sure how teepees and royalty are associated. I'm just reporting here. But you get the idea. I associate the teepee with both my home and my heart.

Afterward, I remembered a Rumi poem inviting us to treat all of our own thoughts and feelings, no matter how unsavory, as welcome guests.

> *This being human is a guest house.*
> *Every morning a new arrival.*
> *A joy, a depression, a meanness,*
> *some momentary awareness comes*
> *as an unexpected visitor.*
> *Welcome and entertain them all!*
> *Even if they are a crowd of sorrows,*
> *who violently sweep your house*
> *empty of its furniture,*
> *still, treat each guest honourably.*
> *He may be clearing you out*
> *for some new delight.*
> *The dark thought, the shame, the malice.*
> *Meet them at the door laughing and invite them in.*
> *Be grateful for whatever comes.*
> *because each has been sent*
> *as a guide from beyond.*

It's good to remember that we need to be hospitable with our own feelings, "the dark thought, the shame, the malice," trusting that on their visit into conscious awareness they come bearing gifts. Impeccable hospitality requires a fundamental trust that every thing and every person who comes into our life is a manifestation, made in the image of Source, regardless of how life circumstances have concealed their deepest identity.

It is equally true that hospitality — the willingness to suffer (accept) reality with equanimity and openness, means receiving with grace the feelings of the other without trying to change them. We can be inhospitable to our children's feelings when, for example, they need to express hatred for us, or rage or sadness. A client recently shared that he found one of his children difficult. The child would express fears of death. He naturally thought that it was his job to cheer her up. Together, we wondered about the possibility of containing her feelings by allowing and receiving them in love. Receiving the feelings of my beloved is particularly challenging for me, especially when I interpret her feelings as meaning that there is something wrong with me. If we have not learned to welcome all of our own feelings into the home of self, we will impulsively slam the door shut when others arrive with their own unruly feelings.

Reminding Those You Meet of Their Royal Status

The people we encounter as we go about our lives have forgotten their royal status. At least, this is true of me. It is, to use Levinas's term, the "face" of the other in their vulnerability that commands my hospitality. It is their vulnerability and forgetting that "elects" us to remind them of their intrinsic worthiness in the eyes of God/Source. They are "high and lifted up." It becomes both our responsibility and our pleasure to remind them of their deepest identity by how we treat them. We know ourselves how easy it is to forget how beautiful we are.

To be on the receiving end of such hospitality is to remember one's inherent dignity. My wife and I were guests of African elder Malidoma Somé, whose life purpose is to build bridges between the traditional ways of his African village and the West. His mother-in-law welcomed us into their home with a traditional Ethiopian coffee ceremony. She is deaf and mute but had no problem communicating kindness. She roasted green beans over an open flame, then ground them and added cumin, cardamom and coriander spices. The first part of the visit involved simply observing the ceremony. Then she poured, from a traditional brass coffeepot, through a filter made from grasses, a demitasse of the most delicious coffee I have ever tasted. This was done with great solemnity and humility.

Only after the coffee ceremony was complete did the conversation start. The only conversation worth having is one that arises when all the participants are grounded in their royal status.

In the movie *Babette's Feast,* a young counter-revolutionary escapes Paris and finds refuge with Protestant sisters who lead a fundamentalist sect in a remote fishing village ("sisters" as in a community of nuns). The young woman, Babette, has no money but offers to be the sisters' cook. She vastly improves their abstemious fare, while they try to pretend that they are not enjoying the elevated standards. After fourteen years of service, Babette discovers that she has won 10,000 francs with a lottery ticket purchased for her annually by a friend. She spends the entire amount preparing the austere nuns a gourmet feast. The sisters would have had no idea what they were eating were it not for a visiting guest who assures them that he has tasted no finer meal in all of Paris. In fact, he says, it reminds him of a meal he had twenty years earlier at a restaurant called Café Anglais. Babette reveals that she was the head chef at this restaurant prior to the revolution.

Babette's extravagant hospitality ensures that she will spend the rest of her life in poverty. But her true wealth is her generosity. Her impeccable hospitality reminds the sisters of their deeper identity as beloved of God. This abundance is the way of Spirit.

3. Move at the Pace of Life

What's the Rush?

Life has its own rhythm. We either learn to dance to this rhythm and discover the competency of effective movement. Or, we go through life with two left feet. These days, when somebody moves with elegance they are often out of sync with society's rhythms. Such people seem strange to us because they refuse to work themselves to death: They rest when they are tired, move when they feel prompted from within, and work at trades and crafts or in businesses tailor-made for an internal rhythm in sync with life.

Fatigue is the first sign that we are keeping pace, not with our own internal, natural rhythm but with the rhythms of our social, political and economic systems. We become breathless because these rhythms are not natural but rather technological. We have been socialized to this unnatural movement, becoming machine-like as we follow an external mandate to keep up. Eventually, we run down, propped up by regular infusions of caffeine, and if we succumb to illness (the inevitable outcome of denying fatigue), even here we are encouraged by the medical system to recover quickly. We are given drugs and sent home before we are ready. We stimulate ourselves with caffeine. There is no time to recover. And if we took the time we genuinely needed, we'd be out of a job.

Some days I think that my role as psychotherapist is very simple: I am giving people time to catch up with themselves, *their* time and *their* timing. It is our time and our timing that is stolen from us.

Recovering and reclaiming our unique pace of life is challenging because even contemporary birth practices are geared to support not the new arrival, but the timing of doctors and the nurses. In 2014 in Brazil, 82 percent of births were by C-section. By 2018, that figure dropped to 50 percent, still a staggeringly high percentage, reflecting the schedules of the doctors and the hospitals, as well as the brainwashing of women that her natural cycles and those of the infant are not critical.[23] Newborns are still routinely whisked away from their mothers at birth rather than setting them on the mother's tummy and letting them make their first heroic journey toward the nipple. The pacing, from a newborn's perspective, is traumatically fast. Birth experiences set a newborn's default neurological system to live in a technologically driven, efficiency-worshiping society.

This is compounded by the bias of our society that a mother should get back to her "normal" routine as quickly as possible. When I was born mothers were allowed up to a week in the hospital for recovery. Today, they are discharged within a day or two. While there are doulas, midwives and some doctors advocating for mothers and fathers to slow way down for at least for the first year of life, and to be attuned to the rhythms of the baby, mostly these naturally slower rhythms of the infant are ignored. From an early age we are "running on nerves" because we cannot keep up.

When mothers and fathers have "no time" themselves because "time is money" in our technological, profit-driven society, children are continually frustrated by having to adjust to the timing of others. Failures of love (trauma) teach children to be excessively vigilant in reading external cues as to when and how to move and act in the world — in sync with the anxiety of others. Finding our own pace when we've been socialized so effectively away from nature, particularly our own nature, is a deep spiritual practice.

---

23 "Why Most Brazilian Women Get C-Sections," *The Atlantic Magazine*, Olga Khazan, April 14, 2014.

Cranial-Sacral Therapy and the Long Tide

It turns out that there is an underlying pace of life that can be felt. Because of chronic headaches, I was in cranial-sacral therapy for two years. This is a hands-on form of therapy, focusing on the cranium, the spine, the sacrum and the underlying fluids of the body. These fluids, and even the bones of the skull, are in constant, subtle motion, responsive to a rhythmic pulse called the "long tide." It cycles in and out every fifty seconds. As the therapist comes into coherence with this tide, the natural health state is supported. You can feel this natural tidal motion when you are still enough.

According to some cranial-sacral therapists, the long tide is a manifestation of the Breath of Life, and it maintains the creative intentions of the Breath of Life no matter what conditions individuals face or how profound their trauma. The long tide itself is never interrupted, just forced to take circuitous pathways.

My description doesn't do this phenomenon justice. But the example of slime mould is perhaps sufficient to support the contention that there is an actual, palpable rhythm or pace of life that underlies all creation. In the 1950s a botanist, William Seifriz, took videos of slime mould as he injected it with various noxious substances. Slime mould is an undifferentiated mass of protoplasm without cell membranes. To his surprise, Seifriz discovered that it was constantly streaming, first one way and then the other, in fifty-second cycles. This streaming was not affected by noxious substances, including anesthetics.

To move with, and be moved by, this rhythm is to come into coherence with life itself. It's no coincidence that the Hebrew word *ruach* means both spirit and breath. A clever theologian didn't just dream this up. We are being breathed by a creative intelligence that brings coherence to chaos, or rather dances with chaos from which life, in its astounding diversity of form, arises.

Yoga is a discipline that focuses on the breath. Turning yourself into a pretzel is secondary. The classes always begin by finding an internal rhythm through the breath. When you enter a posture, you are instructed to only go to a depth where you can maintain the rhythm of the breath. As I observe myself doing the various asanas, I know when I am being willful, pushing myself beyond my capacity, because my breath is short. It is a lesson, of course, for life. What might it look like to live our life without pushing ourselves beyond what the Breath of Life (Long Tide) and our own relaxed breathing allows.

The Chinese term for the Breath of Life is t'ai chi. Tai Chi is a movement practice based on the very subtle principle of Wu wei. It means "not doing" or, even better, "to act without forcing." We can learn to move in alignment with nature's rhythm, whether that's our own nature or creation.

To act without forcing goes against every instinct of the ego, whose job is to make things happen, to engineer the future, to plan, to survive. The last thing our survivor self is interested in is letting our life emerge organically. This would require trust that there is a natural unfolding or flow to life, and that we are being lived by that. The good news is that we truly are being supported unceasingly by this flow.

Strangely, the genesis of the practice of moving at the pace of life is connected to feeling cold. In an ayahuasca ceremony, I notice that my hands and feet are, as usual, freezing. I've always chalked this up to a circulatory problem and to not having much meat on my bones. I am warming my feet up, rubbing them between my hands, when I see how I rush through life. I move at such a pace that my feet and hands aren't actually contacting the world. No contact, no warmth.

Why are we in such a hurry? My first experience of psilocybin (the active ingredient in psychedelic mushrooms) was at a Meat Loaf concert in Winnipeg. I remember coming out of the concert and noticing the traffic whizzing by in all directions. I found all this motion funny and asked out loud: "Where is everybody going in such a hurry?" It seemed clear to me in that moment that we were all just keeping ourselves busy.

Who knows what might happen if we stepped out of the world's rhythm and shifted into a natural rhythm. Most movement is a distraction from deep contact with life, preventing an immersion in it.

Learning to Linger and Making Memories

I don't linger in my experience. Yet lingering is the key to enjoying life. Enjoyment requires time to metabolize experience. This is how memories are made. We allow the world to get through to us, to touch us. We respond. When we make contact, life is warm.

I don't make vivid memories either. Joe, a childhood friend, was a master at making memories. He could regale me with story after story of things that happened when we were growing up which I had completely forgotten about. He could even remember events in my own family that had slipped my memory. I always found this strange. But Joe possessed a basic warmth toward life. I was cooler. He made contact. I skimmed over life, constantly in distracted motion.

Reaching out in curiosity is the origin of movement in babies. But early in life I learned not to reach out, to keep my hands, my mouth, my body to myself. I picked up the message that it wasn't okay to linger in the pleasure of touch. Contact was discouraged, for reasons I may never know.

Having unconsciously perceived the world as unsafe to contact, my alternative was to transition from one thing to another, one thought to another, one experience to the next and one person to another as quickly as possible. Some people just naturally make slow transitions, lingering appropriately before moving on, and learning to say good-bye in such a way that the experience feels complete. But to do this, you need to know that it is safe to linger and stay "in touch" until it truly is time to move.

My wife is amazed by how quickly I'm on to the next thing. In contrast, I watch her with her girlfriends as they take their leave. Saying good-bye is a ten-minute ritual.

I learned to do three or four things at once. I became a multitasker, my hands and feet moving in different directions at the same time. It served me well when I was a waiter. The good nights were when the restaurant was slammed and I had seven or eight tables going. Ringing in the orders while keeping an eye on whether my food was up, barking at the cooks and remembering that somebody asked me for ketchup — this was a good time.

But one of my fellow waiters seemed to go about it differently. Even though he was serving as many tables as me, he moved with grace and presence. He seemed to be all in one place, even though he had as many balls in the air. After work one night he told me that he was a practicing Buddhist. We sat down on a bench near Ryerson College in Toronto. His stillness was palpable. He offered to give me a head massage right there in the public square.

Mindfulness

Later, I would come to know his practice as mindfulness, which is the art of being in your experience. I like Jon Kabat-Zinn's definition of mindfulness: "Mindfulness means paying attention in a particular way; On purpose, in the present moment, and nonjudgmentally." This is similar to what I mean by extending hospitality to all thoughts and feelings, even the so-called negative ones, as if they were honoured guests.

We can bring mindfulness to the way we move through life. Moving at the pace of life, no faster or slower, means moving through life in such a way that we don't get lost in distraction. Distraction, by definition, is a loss of conscious awareness. It means we are allowing our mind and body to disconnect or separate from the experience we're having. For me, this usually involves thinking, unconsciously, about the past or the future. We can think consciously about the past and the future of course. It's just that if I'm doing so while I'm making love with my wife, I'm dissociating. Mindfulness is an antidote to the robot I mentioned earlier. When we fully concentrate our minds on what is happening in the present moment, we take control of the robot.

Distraction is unconscious movement, always away from the present moment and always away from contact with life here and now. If we are doing this habitually, it is because of trauma. We learned that it is not safe to make contact or be present in this moment. If the pleasure of being in the moment is repeatedly interrupted, this registers in our nervous system as pain and suffering. As adults, lingering triggers the memory of being interrupted. We move compulsively as a flight from the memory. In my case, I became stillness averse.

The Dream of a Beautiful Woman

My mother told me that when I was three, the family was traveling to visit cousins in Saskatchewan. I had fallen asleep in the car. I woke up and announced that I'd had a dream: "I dreamed that I got to touch the most beautiful woman in the world."

My hunch is that this dream reflected my longing to touch, and linger in the contact with, my own mother. I feel heartbroken that this wasn't received as a plea for contact.

I'm lying in ceremony, warming my cold feet. I fall in love with my feet, and with the hands that are warming them. I see why they are always cold and make a promise to slow down, tune in and let them have contact with the beautiful world.

4. Leave the Rest to Me

The Self as Ecosystem

The final practice was "Leave the rest to me." "Me" here refers to Source.

I smiled when I heard this one. Though it sounds simple, it's anything but in practice. It requires the death of my belief in, and enactment of, my "self" as a discrete entity separate from everything else. I found this funny because I recognized that in my adapted, egoic self, I truly believed that life was all up to me. And by "me," I meant my own will, disconnected from the larger forces of life that are at play and supporting me 24/7.

This practice relates to the previous one — Move at the Pace of Life — in its recognition that I am being breathed by a creative intelligence that encompasses me, and of which I am a part, but which is also more than me. Life is its own organizing intelligence. I am, you are, one occasion of this intelligence. There are many invisible moving parts, of which we are usually only dimly aware. I am one player in a vast ecosystem of forces at play in my life and with my life — a point of conscious intelligence among multiple centers of intelligence with which I am in relationship. I can only know myself truly and discover my purpose in life by recognizing, respecting and being in relationship with the whole ecosystem of intelligences, seen and unseen.

For example, some indigenous peoples have a dynamic relationship with "the ancestors." The souls of these departed are intimately involved in the unfolding of life on earth, so it is important to stay in good relationship with them. Many indigenous peoples also feel a relationship to the land, sky, air, fire and all sentient creatures. These centers of intelligence are known as "all my relations," and life can only proceed in harmony if the relationship is strong and clean. There exists no "self" separate from these relationships. This explains the emphasis on ceremony in some indigenous cultures. Contrary to popular Western belief that these ceremonies are a fear-based strategy to control nature, they are in fact expressions of gratitude and a means of opening to these various centers of intelligence.

Astrologers throughout the ages have recognized that the way stars, planets and the moon line up at the time of our birth influences our lives in particular ways, and it's important to know details of these alignments when making critical life decisions. The stars, planets and moon participate in the expression of a vast intelligence synchronized with our own life. The movement of the stars and the alignment of the planets are also part of me.

Again, we are all affected by a twenty-four-hour internal clock, the circadian rhythm, that determines when we feel most awake and most tired, generally in response to light and darkness. If we mess with this internal rhythm too much, we will become exhausted.

Along with our human relations, these are just a few of the natural and spiritual, visible and invisible forces that we are embedded in and expressions of. The more of these that we can be in conscious relationship with, the truer an ecosystemic self we will express. We can break out of the illusion of isolation and the independent ego. We will know more deeply, and be in gratitude to, these forces that support our life. Those we recognize as wisdom teachers stay in conscious relationship with these seen and unseen intelligences.

In contrast, the more unintegrated trauma we carry, the more we will feel unsupported and isolated, heroically forging our way in a mechanistic universe, devoid of any intrinsic purpose, meaning, intelligence — and natural flow. Sadly, the worldview of scientific materialism (which reduces everything to mechanical bits of unintelligent matter) supports this idea of the self, and is itself a reflection of it.

The endless "search for self" is a modern phenomenon that is, in part, the inevitable result of the evolution of consciousness. When humans gained the capacity to distinguish between a mind "in here" and a world "out there," the self and the mind were experienced as separate from the world for the first time in human history. Eventually, given the modernist impulse to rid the world of all forces that can't be measured and controlled for (in particular, God), the self became increasingly isolated and disconnected. Late postmodernist philosophy contends that humans are centers of meaning and purpose in an inanimate universe devoid of value. In this view, even the meaning we make is believed to be an arbitrary construction. No wonder we feel lost. We are among the first generations to seriously entertain the possibility that we are islands of meaning in a vast and expanding ocean of meaninglessness.

The pervasive loneliness in contemporary society and our endless search for self reflect a longing to connect with these invisible forces. There is truly no self apart from these connections.

A New Take On Surrender

To surrender, then, means to surrender into the radical interconnectedness of reality, to relax into this vast network of relationships and invisible forces, and to sacrifice our isolation and the attendant suffering it causes. It means to trust that all of these forces are in some unfathomable way *for* us and will guide our path naturally and organically, if we could only relax. This is the way of the Tao.

To surrender does not mean relinquishing our authentic will. It does not mean submission. It means letting go of, dying to, the will that is an expression of our false (traumatized) self. It means letting go of the perception of an isolated self and dropping into a relational self, or what I've called the ecosystemic self. As we participate consciously in many cosmic, social and natural forces that constitute us, and as we are participated by them, a more robust, relational self emerges.

The self is neither lost nor relinquished in surrender. It expands into its deeper and broader identity, a localized center of consciousness expressing its unique gifts on behalf of the whole ecosystem of intelligences. When we express our will from our essential, connected nature, the result is an expression of the Whole.

This is the only expression of self that can be trusted, because the isolated ego is the traumatized ego. It cannot help but live out its life in a disconnected, and therefore violent, manner. This is what we see happening in the world today.

When we surrender the isolated self into a condition of communion with the Whole, we fulfill our distinct identity and purpose as a node of consciousness, dedicated to serving the Whole in love.

CHAPTER 15

Bearing Intensity

All In

I've taken MDMA and LSD. My connection with my therapist is intense. It feels like everything is on the line, as though the whole of the universe is present right here, right now, in our connection. This is what I want, what I've always wanted. It's what I am in flight from, what I've always been in flight from. I can't bear it. I must bear it. It's all there is. It's why I showed up in the first place.

So this is what life feels like when I'm "all in." When a poker player feels like the cards have landed in his favour, he shoves all of his chips into the center of the table. He's betting the farm on his hand. This is what it feels like right now. There's a sense that I can't lose. Or if I do lose, it's okay. To not make the bet would be crazy. It feels like this is the only game in town.

It's hard for adults who have not been taken seriously as children to appreciate how intensely infants, toddlers and adolescents experience their sensations and feelings. Alice Miller demonstrates in case after case how parents will actually shame small children and adolescents for exhibiting frustration, devastation, rage, joy, love, grief and other emotions. This is because they were themselves denied the free expression of these feelings and sensations, and to see them arise in their own children creates anxiety. Unconsciously, parents shut down the feelings and impulses of their children to relieve their own anxiety. When this happens, the gift of intensity is stolen from the children.

It is this original capacity to feel reality with intensity that comes back online on psychedelics. In his book on the phenomenology of the ayahuasca experience, Benny Shanon writes that the most common description by those who take this medicine is that it is "more real than real."[24]

Intensity is the experience of the absolute value of life.

The Russian novelist Dostoyevsky discovered this intensity when he was unexpectedly given a reprieve from execution. From that moment on, he never let himself retreat into a state of indifference about life.

Colin Wilson writes about what he calls the "indifference threshold." This refers to how low or high we set the bar relative to the absolute value of life. Murderers set it extremely low. What is sobering to me is that while I hadn't set the bar murderously low, when I looked at where it was relative to how I felt on psychedelics, it was pretty low. On the medicine I realized just how much everything mattered, what a gift life is, and what a travesty it was to hold myself back from being penetrated by it all. Numbing oneself so as not to be penetrated by life is a common legacy of emotional, physical or sexual trauma — we've learned that it's safer to not be penetrated.

Wilson believes that laziness and weak-mindedness cause us to relinquish intensity. But he missed the impact of trauma. I've seen for myself how the unambiguous feeling of the absolute value of life gave way to dis-

---

24 Benny Shanon, *Antipodes of the Mind: Charting the Phenomenology of the Ayahuasca Experience* (Oxford: Oxford University Press, 2002).

appointment. I saw how I was forced to give up intensity as a child. When children overwhelm their parents with feelings (because the parents themselves were forced to suppress these feelings when they were children), the parents find ways to teach children that such feelings are unacceptable. In this way, unconsciously, the parents avoid the punishment they received as children.

The most common strategy is to shame the child. Shame and humiliation are the most painful of all feelings to bear, so the child will quickly learn to construct a false self. Shame makes us want to disappear from the world. It is an intensity killer because it teaches us that feelings are unbearable. And then we generalize that belief to all of life. *Life is too much to bear.* We harden our bodies, dampen our nervous systems and close our hearts so that life doesn't affect us. In the process we sacrifice intensity.

When we lose a feeling for the absolute value of life, our intellect may develop at the expense of our emotional life. As Miller points out, this emotional detachment "is no obstacle to the development of intellectual abilities, but it is one to the unfolding of an authentic emotional life."[25]

In fact, these increased intellectual capacities will be recruited to justify, consolidate and defend the false self. I have caught myself developing elaborate philosophical theories to this end. I am convinced that professional philosophers develop entire systems of thought and worldviews as abstract and unconscious response to early trauma. Existentialist philosophers, whose own lives often ended in misery and addiction, wrote philosophies of despair. What is required, they contend, is courage to face the emptiness of existence. But existence isn't actually empty. They are describing lost intensity — intensity lost in response to being punished, ignored or shamed when feelings and sensations were too intense for the parent to bear.

Most addictions start out as a strategy to recapture lost intensity. At least in the beginning, the substance that alters consciousness bypasses the defenses, and the person regains some of the intensity of feeling that has been lost to the false self. After a few drinks, the friendly drunk is professing undying love for the stranger at the bar. Or he may express sadness or

---

25 Alice Miller, *The Drama of the Gifted Child: The Search for the True Self* (New York: Basic Books, 1981).

anger. But in the beginning, before the booze or the cocaine becomes a prison, it is liberating.

Repetitive suffering can also be an attempt to regain a sense of the absolute value of life. We can fall in love with suffering because at least it recaptures intensity. Repetitive compulsion is, by definition, the unconscious re-creation of circumstances that cause us suffering. But this kind of suffering, while intense, is self-destructive, not life-giving. We are enacting upon ourselves what was done to us. In therapy, the goal is to exit this negative intensity directed against the self so that we can recover authentic feelings that belong to the present.

When we learn that it is not safe to be "all in," we are forced to live outside our bodies. Our false self carries us for a time. Instead of feeling life, we vacillate between grandiosity — pretending to be more than who we actually are to please the mother or father who cannot accept us unconditionally — and depression. When the grandiose strategies of being super competent, super together, super kind, super effective, super smart, super everything fail, depression sets in because we don't actually have a self to help us navigate life. The old forgotten feelings of helplessness and sorrow for not being known or seen rise up anew. My therapist, Andrew, defines what we call "depression" as a combination of lack of self-expression and oppression.

During one ayahuasca ceremony I recall coming down out of my grandiosity and saying out loud, "I'm just Bruce. I'm not special. I don't know anything. I have nothing to give you. Just myself." It was the sad voice of a very young child who had learned that to be loved he needed to be special.

In another ceremony I saw that all the suffering in the room was the result of the participants' belief that they could not be themselves.

Because I was so "successful" in life (my grandiose compensation), my bouts of depression and moodiness seemed totally random and mysterious. In our society, when we pop out of our grandiose self and tell our friendly GP about feeling depressed, she won't hesitate to chalk it up to a chemical imbalance and prescribe an antidepressant. The irony is that these drugs merely mask the underlying trauma, supporting our repression and denial.

Limbo

In an LSD and MDMA session, I see clearly that I am hanging out in no-man's-land, neither all in nor all out. By "all out" I mean that I hadn't checked out. I hadn't killed myself, which is always an option. If I wasn't in, then why not exit?

This is a very real question on the medicine, which may scare the shit out of most people reading this — confirming that psychedelics are dangerous. They aren't. But they do open one up to the intensity of life. No more bullshit. Either commit to life or throw in the towel.

That's when I realize I spend a whole lot of time *pretending* that I am not all in. I want to live. I intuitively know, however, that to truly commit to life — to get out of the neutral zone — is to face my old, old heartbreak.

A long time ago, when I discovered that I could not be myself, I entered limbo. I decided to hang out in this space until it was safe to come back. Only, I forgot to come back. I forgot because, in my grandiose "successful" self, I was checking all the boxes for what constituted a "good" life. I had to leave the church, a marriage, financial security, and I had to find my soul mate, to see that it was time to shit or get off the pot. It was time to rejoin life, which meant allowing the intensity of feelings and sensations to return. It meant falling back in love with life.

"Being here" means feeling life in all its intensity. It means showing up, trusting that there is actually no "bad" experience. There is only experience. It's important for me to remember that when life feels gray and flat, it is a memory. I am "graying" and "flattening" myself. I learned that flat and grey was relatively safe, but these are not feelings. They are the world my perceptual system creates when I refuse to feel. And this refusal to feel, once a necessary defense mechanism, became a habit. I will default to the state of the dull limbo under stress.

But the medicine temporarily suspends this defense system. It shows me what life actually feels like: I'm here. You are there. It's so intense to actually connect as two "others." There is so much curiosity, so much anticipation, so much not knowing and wanting to know, so much love, so much fear of being hurt, so much trust, so much joy in realizing that you are choosing not to hurt me. You could destroy me, but you are letting me be. Letting me be exactly who I am. If you are not, it hurts. But I now know what I didn't know then: that you cannot destroy me. I discover that my heart actually feels, it moves, opens, expands and contracts. I feel my heart opening to you and to life.

Too Good to Be True?

During this same session, I spontaneously break into a comedy act.

Two old guys are lying on the beach. Harry is drinking a margarita through a straw. He turns to his buddy, Frank, and says, "Hey, Frank, have you ever wondered if this is all there is to it? I mean, two guys lying on a beach, scratching their balls, pulling down a government pension? We have everything we need right here."

Frank shrugs his shoulders and tells Harry that, just in case, they had better keep it to themselves. If anybody found out, they might take away their pension or make them come home and go to work. "Just keep it quiet," says Frank. "Maybe nobody will find out."

The Law of the Pendulum

I am reminded of the Rumi quote "It's rigged. Everything is in your favour!"

This doesn't mean that life always swings our way. Life brings what it brings. But it's all in the service of more abundance.

I receive another email from somebody promising eternal peace, lasting abundance, continual health and unending prosperity if I just sign up for yet another program. The problem with these promises is that this isn't how life works. Life isn't constant. It's not a steady state. If we believe that a truly spiritual person never experiences scarcity, illness or chaos, the presence of these "bad" conditions in our own life causes us to feel that something must be wrong, either with ourselves or with life itself. We become attached to some life conditions as "good" and others as "bad." The result is that we are externally conditioned, taking our cues from what life hands us and then reacting to these conditions. But we are on the wrong end of a yo-yo, scrambling to recreate the "good" conditions, or worrying that we have fallen from the ideal state.

Gurdjieff teaches the Law of the Pendulum, which seems eminently more sensible. Life swings between opposites. Sometimes abundance.

Sometimes scarcity. Sometime peace. Sometimes chaos. But there is a center point between the swings of the pendulum. At this still point, our true "I" arises.

We are at peace at both extremes of the pendulum because our true "I" is not conditioned by the swings. Rather, our true, unified "I" conditions life. (If we are conditioned by those swings, then life is conditioning us.) When Jesus said of John the Baptist that he was not a "reed blowing in the wind," he meant that John was not conditioned by, or identified with, life conditions.

When Job was tested by "the Satan" and everything was removed from him — his wealth, his health, his friends — this is what was being tested. Was he externally conditioned? Or, had he gained sufficient self-coherence that he could watch the pendulum swing without reacting at either extreme? In the end, Job realized that he was distinct from life conditions and circumstances. "Now the eyes of my eyes see..."

Life is "rigged" in the sense that every condition of life is a perfect opportunity to manifest our essential nature rather than be blown about by circumstance.

What if all we need to do is show up, moment by moment, without any distractions, feel what there is to feel and be on the receiving end of a universe that is for us? What if life is actually so unambiguously good that we can't believe it or accept it?

I see how, as a species, we organize our entire lives, entire epochs and civilizations, to create distractions from the possibility that it's all rigged from the get-go in our favour. If we were to all come to this realization, the artificial constructs built on distracting ourselves from the essential goodness of life would come tumbling down. It would be the end of civilization as we know it. What if life isn't a problem to be solved but a mystery to be inhabited fully? The medicine gave me a glimpse into a world of simplicity, abundance and pleasure — regardless of circumstance.

Pop Goes the Heart

It doesn't mean that there is no heartbreak. But as Rilke puts it, "Just keep going. No feeling is final." Intensity is the willingness to feel everything.

It's how the human heart expands over a lifetime or many lifetimes into the divine heart.

When I came out of the session I told my wife what I had learned about the intensity of life. Then I riffed on how the purpose of intensity is to expand the heart. When the feelings get too intense, the heart expands and goes "pop." It breaks open and grows larger to increase its capacity for intensity. With this increased capacity, the heart can take more direct experience of intensity — of truth, beauty, goodness, sorrow, and the rest — and then, "pop," it breaks open again. This is the evolution of heart intelligence.

I saw that each time the heart "pops" and reconstitutes itself to feel more intensity, we bring forth a new world, a world in which we can see more and more of what is already present. Seeing more and feeling more of the intensity, we create new possibilities for our own lives.

Is this how the universe came into being in the first place? Did Source's heart overflow with an intensity of love for the possibility of others inhabiting the universe? In that intensity the divine heart broke, letting loose the overflowing creativity and love that became the universe. This continues to happen moment by moment, in and through the hearts of those willing to bear this intensity.

Is this also the core meaning of the Sacred Heart of Jesus? Here is a human willing to bear the intensity of life. His heart breaks open on the cross, but from his willingness to suffer, a new creation pours forth from his broken heart. To reenact this pattern is to get to the "crux" (cross) of the matter. It is to go to the cross, moment by moment, because it requires the death of our defended ego. And every death of this defended self is at the same time a new creation, a resurrection of life's potential.

Love Everything You Do
The world is there to be loved
If you love everything you do
the world lights up.
You have one thousand
excuses
for why you can't love
everything you do.
I know.

I have used them all
to keep myself miserable.
When your house is built upon
these excuses
the power goes out,
and you spend all your time
cursing the darkness.
The world becomes
empty and meaningless.
Philosophers write books
telling you that this is the real world,
and will give you a prize
for bothering to get out of bed.
Don't be fooled by the academics of doom
nor by the dewy-eyed mystics
who have never risked the darkness.

Love everything you do.
I mean right now.
Everything is contained
in this moment.
Everything.
All your loves, sorrows, hatreds and joys.
You can only love this moment
by being in it,
embracing whatever the moment holds.
The moment can be held like you would a baby.
Why would you look away,
or escape it with distraction?
Why want to be somewhere else?
Take that question seriously, now.
Your lost life is in there somewhere.
I'll wait.

Truly, there is no way out of this moment,
or the next

or the next.
There is only the hell of the secret exit
from the boring conversation,
from letting love drive you deep,
from the weight of sorrow
and the arresting beauty.
There are a thousand escape hatches
in your repertoire of fear.
Naming them is spiritual practice.

There is also the heaven
of facing the truth,
and declaring your outrage
as you push back your chair
from the table
and just leave,
like a sage.

While you're at it
leave the friendship,
the job,
the marriage,
the party,
the sermon,
the deal,
the family,
the covenant of nice
before it's too late.
Love it or leave it.
What I am proposing
is more radical than you think.
It will leave your life in shambles.
It is death to your so-called life.
Love everything you do.

Take up arms

against boredom.
Endure nothing and nobody.
No excuses.
Your "no" must be absolute
before you can find your "yes."

Soon, people will run
when they see you coming
if they have not broken
the polite covenant themselves,
if they have settled for misery.
Your true friends
are those who are left
after the room empties,
who smile when they see
you coming,
and can't wait to enter
into the intensity of what is,
now,
arising,
the eternity of every moment
where there are no rules,
no roles,
only the knowing of what is right for each you,
where nothing is predictable,
where the universe is born again.

Once you did love everything,
with all your heart
before it was broken,
by failures of love

There is the terrible hopelessness
of knowing that you were forced
to make a promise
to never be yourself.

You wore this agreement around you
like a shroud that let no light in.

Now you know that there was nothing,
nothing, you could have done.
Don't tell me the darkness isn't real.
It's terrible.
This is when you started looking for the exit sign,
when the love you felt for everything
and the heartbreak
became entwined.
You, the great and noble survivor,
learned the art of distraction,
from both the hopelessness
and the threat of love.
You put them under day arrest.
But they come for you
in your nightmares,
and the way you distrust the ones
you love the most.

One day,
if you are lucky,
you will gaze upon the ruins of your life,
and discover that
it was mostly distraction anyway,
that it has not been your
life you had been living.
And you see
that this is why you
cannot risk being in every moment,
or trust your longing.

You learned well the lesson,
to pretend you didn't care,
to reduce the intensity

that was you,
to save your life.
You don't remember your life because
It didn't matter.
You didn't matter.
Life was dulled and dimmed
and then you learned
to dull and dim.

It is now time for Grief
to come and take your hand.
Courage, my friend.
Let your heart break.
Take grief's hand.
She is too wise a guide
to feel sorry for you.
She is giving you back your life.

It is time to go to that place
where there was neither love
or light.
It's time to face the hopelessness
and feel again
that there is no escape.
Nobody can assure you
that it is not true.
You can only discover it
for yourself.

The moaning you hear
is not that of a stranger.
You are making these
terrible sounds,
cries of freedom, resurrection, and rage.
This forbidden howling
that you've hidden

beneath shallow breathing,
abstract ideals,
and a swollen intellect.

This is the intensity
of the present moment
what you want
and fear most,
the reason for your love affair
with distraction.
This is the cross,
the crux of the matter,
the excruciating breaking of the heart.
This is you, finally, blessedly.

The next voice you hear
will be your own
speaking to the little one within,
telling him that he can come to you
in his sadness,
with his hopelessness,
with all the love he has for the world
and wasn't able to give.
He can make memories again.

It is you now,
the Great Mother,
offering full breasts
weeping for the little one
you hold with such love.
The light shines in the darkness,
and the darkness has not overcome it.
Love everything you do.

CHAPTER 16

The Trauma Signature

Neurosis…is the process of reliving rather than living, choosing bondage over freedom, the old over the new, the past over now. It is the attempt to create a parent or parents in other persons, institutions or if all else fails, in oneself…In other words one clings to the emotional deadness of family and to its illusions of safety and security by repeating early patterns with new objects.
— **Robert Firestone, *The Fantasy Bond***

Core Unconscious Beliefs (CUBs): The Shadow

In response to early childhood trauma, we form core unconscious beliefs (CUBs) about ourselves and the world. These beliefs create the self we believe to be our true self but isn't. We create our life by enacting these beliefs. They were originally unpleasant or even unbearable body sensations that we translate into meaning about the self and the world.

These beliefs are negative, self-destructive and self-sabotaging. But they form the interpretive filtering system through which all events, circumstances and conditions of our life must pass. Even though we create our reality through them, because they are unconscious we cannot own them. In this sense, they prevent us from taking responsibility for our lives.

These CUBs (along with our CABs, which I discuss below) limit our potential, keep us stuck in a negative feedback loop and ensure that we reenact our traumatic history. When these beliefs are in place, we will default to them under stress or when we are triggered by an external event or relationship. We cannot help but become reactive under conditions and circumstances that challenge or confirm these beliefs.

For example, if my CUB "I am bad" is challenged by loving gestures from my wife, I may mysteriously react negatively. I may experience an impulsive (unconscious) desire to isolate myself and not let the feeling of being worthy register. Or I will outright reject her. This is because, as we've seen, I formed a threshold related to my capacity to receive love based on my CUB. My wife's gestures threaten the defense system I've put in place to prevent anyone crossing the threshold.

The alternative is more painful but more real. I could let her love reach me, feel the grief associated with the trauma of not being loved, and establish a new, higher threshold. This is possible, though it rarely happens. Summoning the self-reflection and self-compassion to overcome the anxiety that arises when we allow the defense system to stand down long enough to make room for new behavior requires a heroic journey.

These CUBs program our lives. If they remain unconscious we are robots, either enacting them directly by making poor decisions or covering them up by compensating with our false self.

These unconscious beliefs, along with the feelings and behaviors associated with them, form the self that we commit to. We invest in this self, habituating to its moods, attitudes and behaviors. Even when they do not serve us well, their familiarity draws us to align ourselves with them. We may repeatedly hurt those we love in this expression of self. But we will not change because this signature is chiseled into our energetic field. To default to it feels like coming home. This is our trauma signature.

The Trauma Signature

We construct an elaborate defense system — compensatory actions and beliefs (CABs, described in the next section) — so that trauma and the associated beliefs will not be exposed. These CABs were formed unconsciously when we could not have survived without them. We continue to believe this is true.

Because they are unconscious, and because we compulsively defend these beliefs when they are threatened, getting at our CUBs is difficult. Most people never understand that they are driven by these beliefs. This is sad. It is impossible to evolve in freedom or to contribute to the evolution of human culture when we are driven by unconscious negative beliefs.

If freedom is defined as consumer choice — the freedom to choose the red one over the green one — then, yes, to this limited degree we are free. But true freedom, which is the capacity to make choices that are not determined by any unconscious factors, is beyond us if we have not identified our CUBs.

What follows is a partial list of my own CUBs. These are in no way abstract or made up. I know the signature of each one of them, and I have learned to know when I am in the grip of each belief:

I am bad.
I am not enough.
I am too much.
I am the cause of your misery.
I cannot have what I want.
My needs are wrong.
I can't love.
I am not loveable. (You don't really love me.)
I don't belong.
Life sucks.
I am stupid.
I am hopeless (the situation is hopeless).
I can't support myself.
I am helpless.
It's my fault.
I am motherless.
I will be killed if I don't do what you want.
Life is meaningless.
I am not safe.

Before working with LSD, MDMA and ayahuasca I would have denied every one of these beliefs, except the first one. I uncovered the belief that "I am bad" when I was in therapy at twenty-nine. But these beliefs became clear the more I worked with the medicine. As mentioned, each of these CUBS has its own signature — that is, each has its own way of showing up in my life and sabotaging me. Each has its own triggers. And each has its associated moods, feelings and preferred behaviors. The composite of all of them is what I'm calling the trauma signature.

These beliefs are not natural. We are not born with them. The foundation of each of these beliefs is shame. We learned that we could not relax and respond to life spontaneously and naturally and be loved. Shame makes us feel like we want to disappear. We do not want to be seen by anybody, and we may spend a lifetime hiding our true self from everyone, including our self, because we learned that to express this self is to be humiliated.

Nobody, of their own volition, believes that they are bad, unlovable or stupid. But I hope I've shown how, faced with the choice of seeing my parents as bad or myself as bad, I'll assume that I'm bad every time. It is mandatory that I form a belief that *I* must be bad, and that it is *all my fault*.

At the end of the film *Good Will Hunting*, Will is remembering how his father physically beat him. His father set out three objects he intended to beat Will with and then made him choose. Will chose the object that would inflict the most pain. When his therapist asks why, Will says: "Because, fuck him." In other words, as a protest, Will made himself immune to his father's violence.

His therapist tells him, "It's not your fault. It's not your fault."

You can see the anxiety rising in Will, because his therapist is breaking through his defense system. Will's promise to himself that he will never let his true feelings show is threatened. He's also about to see that he wasn't bad. In reality, his father was a monster. Letting his therapist in means letting the whole truth in. He breaks down in his therapist's arms, sobbing.

The assignment of personal responsibility for what happened gives one the illusion of control. If *they* are bad, I'm screwed. My life is absolutely contingent. If I'm bad, though, I can do something. I can be good. I can be better. I can find ways to please. I can try harder. Letting go of this belief, then, means accepting that the situation, and my very life, is beyond my control. I'd rather be the cause of being hurt than accept that acts of violence and lovelessness are either completely arbitrary or executed by those on whom I am absolutely dependent.

Incidentally, these CUBS render the new age love affair with positive affirmation almost useless. I can affirm that "I am beautiful" until I'm blue in the face. But these deeper unconscious beliefs that constitute my trauma signature will trump positive affirmations every time. As long as they are in place, affirmations don't have a chance.

Compensating Actions and Beliefs (CABs): The False Self

Both the trauma that causes us to form these beliefs, and the beliefs themselves, are too painful for a child to integrate. Therefore, they become unconscious and we find ways to compensate. We do this, if we are able, through compensating actions and beliefs (CABs).

We can think about CABs as a transport system, our way of getting around in life. It's like calling a taxi because we don't have our own car to navigate through life. Our own car would be our spontaneous, natural and intuitive impulses — a trauma-free self. Most of us, however, were taught to be frightened of driving our own car.

If we lived through our CUBS we would get nowhere. It would be like a traffic jam 24/7. We would be depressed, anxious, compulsive, withdrawn, powerless, and we would lack sufficient vitality to take care of the basic necessities. This is why we need CABs to navigate our life in the presence of trauma. The problem is that once they are formed, they last a lifetime. This is our false self, showing up as very precise compensating beliefs and actions.

For example, I formed a belief that I was too much. There was something about me that overwhelmed my mother. So I formed a compensatory belief that needing anything from life is wrong and dangerous. By the time I reached adulthood, my capacity to know that I had needs, let alone my ability to articulate them, was severely compromised. The corresponding action was that I became hypersensitive about not being welcome — especially when I was in a vulnerable position, such as being comforted. For example, my wife was cuddling me the other morning. She shifted her body to get more comfortable and I jumped away from her — clearly a memory. I interpreted her movement as rejection of my need.

Here's a chart, a snapshot, of how my own CUBS and CABs work together.

Core Unconscious Beliefs (Shadow)	Compensatory Action and Beliefs (False Self)
I am bad.	I am a "very good" boy. I idealize my mother.
I am too much.	Needing is bad. I don't ask for help. I am hypersensitive to cues that I'm asking too much.
I am not enough.	I am perfect. I must be adequate in all situations.
I am helpless.	I am self-sufficient, needing nobody.
It's my fault.	I am right.
Somebody will rescue me.	I don't need anybody.
I'm unlovable.	I am special and exceptional.
Life is meaningless.	Meaning is found in systems of ideas.
My mother will kill me if I don't behave.	I am invulnerable. I cannot be hurt.
I am motherless.	My mother is the best mother ever. She truly loves me. She gave everything for me.
I'm incapable of love.	Love is everything. Love becomes the foundation of my spirituality.
I can't support myself.	I am self-sufficient.
I am without hope.	It could be worse. I'm okay. Look on the bright side.
I am stupid.	I must know everything in a perfect way before I speak up. I hide my stupidity behind intellectualism.
Life sucks.	There is a way out. I pretend to be present when I'm not really. I pretend that I'm engaged when I'm not.
I don't belong.	To belong I must be exceptional, the leader. I compulsively check to make sure I'm invited/I have the right time.
I can't have what I want.	I get what I want only by being indirect, through strategy and manipulation.
I am the cause of your misery.	I am never the cause of anybody's misery. I flee, or emotionally cut off, from others' deep pain and suffering.
I am unsafe.	Nothing bothers me. I am not affected by you. I can take it.

As you can see, this false self is the defense system built right into our personality. It is defended so strongly because the alternative is to collapse into the CUBs. To see the CUBs, in turn, is to open to grief, but this grief was too much when we were going through it the first time. Our CABs protected us at one point. But as adults they sap vitality, joy and intensity.

Leaks

Below is a chart of what happens when my CUBs break through the false self and are expressed more directly. Keep in mind, this expression is still unconscious. I call these expressions of self "leaks." These are more congruent with my CUBs than my CABs are, but they are still unconscious expressions. For example, I may go into periods of deep sadness but not understand that I am expressing my belief that I am motherless. If my CAB can't hold, the original wound leaks out.

With leaks, the feelings and behaviors that would have been appropriate responses to trauma when I was a child now seep through the defense system that is the false self. We are in a regressed state, taken back to our childhood, and we are attempting to let the world know about our suffering, hoping that somebody will see us and comfort us. Suicidal thoughts, gestures and attempts are extreme examples of leaks. Immersed in a memory of a time when life was intolerable, we can see no other way out.

But because we do not understand where these leaks come from, we feel victimized by feelings over which we seem to have no control. We might go to a psychiatrist, who may treat the symptoms with an anti-depressant. We might even put ourselves in a hospital to manifest our feeling of helplessness. But unless psychiatrists or doctors are aware of the effects of trauma, the cause will remain untouched.

Here is a chart of how I act out my CUBs when my CABs leak.

Core Unconscious Beliefs	Leaks
I am bad.	Depression and shame.
I am too much.	I suppress emotions, thoughts and will. I go flat.
I am not enough.	I lash out when somebody or some circumstance confirms my core belief of inadequacy. I exhibit a lack of imagination in the face of challenge.
I am helpless.	Under stress I collapse. I get stuck in life. I lack imagination to conceive alternatives.
It's my fault.	I assume too much responsibility for others and too quickly.
Somebody will rescue me (pick up my inner baby/inner toddler).	I passively orient to difficult situations. I wait to be rescued by something or somebody external to me.
I'm unlovable.	Shame. I isolate myself.
Life is meaningless.	I feel hopeless. I give up and study philosophical systems of despair.
My mother will kill me if I don't behave.	I vaguely feel in danger of being extinguished. I search the environment for cues about what's expected of me and behave accordingly.
I am motherless.	Inconsolable sorrow. Depression. Women exist to mother me. Women become mother and then I reject them.
I'm incapable of love.	Shame. Hopelessness.
I can't support myself.	I secretly get others to support me.
I am without hope.	Depression.
I am stupid.	I don't risk doing a PhD. I never believe that I am smart enough. I rationalize this.
Life sucks.	Suicidal thoughts. Boredom and restlessness.
I don't belong.	I'm an outsider, which I may idealize.
I can't have what I want.	I live through other people's desires because I don't know my own.
I am the cause of your misery.	Impulse to constantly apologize for being who I am. "I'm so sorry for ruining your life."
I am unsafe.	I am sure that you are my enemy, that you are doing things intentionally to hurt me.

These examples show how my beliefs are directly acted out. But if you asked me why I was acting the way I was, I would blame it on some circumstance or the way somebody treated me. When we cannot compensate for the deep wound that created the belief in the first place, feelings and behaviors that are more congruent leak through. The belief "I am motherless" leaks through as sorrow. "Life sucks" leaks through as suicidal fantasies. "I don't belong" can leak through as I walk away from a party that I've been invited to but which overwhelms me at the last moment. "I'm helpless" manifests as moodiness and passivity.

In effect, what happens is that when we feel overwhelmed, these leaks breach the bulwark of the false self (CABS). They return us to the pain of the original trauma. But these leaks that directly express our underlying trauma are rarely recognized as such. We don't "get" why we have suicidal thoughts, feelings of helplessness and depression. It seems to us that we've been sideswiped by life and by circumstances. We feel like we are victims. We are unable to take responsibility for our lives.

Leaks Are Memories

Without some kind of support it is difficult, if not impossible, to appreciate that these leaks, although more direct expressions of underlying trauma than our CUBS, are memories. By "memories" I don't mean specific detailed memories of traumatic events but rather the sensations, feelings, beliefs, thoughts, attitudes and behaviors that represent (re-presence) how we reacted to our lived experience of childhood.[26] The memory of our early trauma is trying to get our attention. But when we are in the clutches of these memories, they overtake us, hijacking our present reality and replacing it with a memory of the sensations surrounding a past event or even just the more general milieu of our family system. We are reacting now as though we are being traumatized in the present. When we are identified with these memories, it takes a lot of discipline, support and experience to take a step back and witness how they are playing out in our lives — to see how we are allowing them to play out *as* our life!

---

26 Sometimes we do remember a specific event, which can be helpful. But it's unnecessary for healing.

Often in ayahuasca circles I have heard guides use the expression "that's just a story" when people describe their suffering. Without nuance, this can come across as lacking in compassion, which is usually not the case. The guides are always compassionate. They know it's important that we realize our early experiences of failures of love are not "just stories." They are real events. The suffering caused is real. What they refer to as a story is the hijacking of our present circumstances by the memory of an original trauma. We may believe that the present circumstances warrant the reaction we are having, but the guides are telling us that we are reacting to a recapitulation or reenactment of the early memory, not to the event that is happening to us now. We get "triggered" in a relationship at home or at work, and we react with emotion and conviction disproportionate to the actual event. This is a memory.

When we learn to hold our CUBs, CABs and "leaks" as memories of intolerable events in our past, our healing begins.

While I was writing this book, I became depressed. I lost vitality. The force of gravity seemed to amplify. My body felt heavy. I struggled to find a reason to get out of bed. I felt hopeless and helpless. I developed a great compassion for those people who struggle with chronic depression. One day, as I walked my dog at the beach, the feeling was so intolerable that I felt I couldn't go on. This had to stop. My wife reminded me that what I was experiencing was a memory. And while I had understood this intellectually, this time it hit me like a tsunami of truth.

I came to see that I had been depressed most of my life, but a combination of hormones and success in sports and in my career had helped me to mask my CUBs. When I started my healing with the help of psychedelics and ayahuasca, the lid came off. My shadow (all the repressed memories and aspects of myself that I judge to be unacceptable) and my false self were exposed by the truth. My life was in full leak mode. The sorrow, hopelessness and feeling of helplessness in the face of it all was now raw and immediate. No denial. No repression. I was fucked.

But it was all a memory. When I truly got this, when I understood it in my spirit and body as well as my intellect, my depression lifted. My energy returned. I even caught myself feeling good from time to time!

We create reality from our trauma signature. The dynamics of every relationship, at work, at home, with our family and friends, are its manifestations. It becomes a kind of alchemical crucible for our life. In it we transform the elements of our life, not to gold, but to shit.

While writing this chapter I watched *The Dinner*, a film about two brothers who have never dealt with their respective childhood traumas at the hands of a mother who could not love them. The younger brother is contending with trauma caused by his mother loving his older brother but not him. (I remember watching the Smothers Brothers, who made a comedy skit from this dynamic.) The older brother is traumatized because he was his mother's confidant and because he carried guilt about his brother's treatment.

The younger brother is obsessed with the Battle of Gettysburg, which was, you'll remember, a family feud writ large on a national level. The southern U.S. states were pitted against the northern states, which wanted to abolish slavery. Through this historical obsession about Gettysburg, the brother externalizes his obsession with what happened in his own family. He is fighting a great battle for justice to be done and for the wrong to be righted. But this obsession with Gettysburg is a projection of his inner battle. He is reenacting the trauma unconsciously.

His trauma "leaks" out as self-hatred, self-destructive gestures (he hits himself), a perpetual harping on the unfairness of life, and violence toward anybody he perceives as being treated as special. He and his wife reenact his early childhood trauma, as his wife has a special and exclusive relationship with their son.

I have spoken about repetition compulsion elsewhere. It is obvious once we've done the work (that is, once we've made all of this past trauma conscious and discovered our deeper signature), that we've created the circumstance of our lives to work this all through. The challenge is that in a state of unconsciousness we will argue vehemently, like the younger brother, that we are victims of a world intent on destroying us. The universe is aligned against us. We will prove our victimhood by pointing out in detail how this conspiracy has been enacted to keep us from being happy, fulfilled and rewarded. We will be the architects of our own destruction and happily blame it on life. Yet it is all a memory.

Trauma as Disease

Our leaks show up in our bodies as disease. The prevailing medical model continues to focus on the alleviation of symptoms, without discerning these symptoms as the language of the body. Bodies don't lie. In my psychedelic journeys I will usually start with a period of violent shaking, focused in the pelvic region. I now understand that I carry my stress, sexual repression and repressed trauma in my pelvis and my hips. My body shakes to release this stored energy, which is now showing up as hip pain and pelvic pain that often keeps me awake at night. If I told my doctor this, he might send me for an appointment with a hip surgeon. Don't get me wrong; I'm grateful for hip replacement surgery and for the surgeons who perform the operation. But I know (in my bones!) that my pelvis and hips are trying to tell me something that could spare me this operation.

Others carry trauma in their stomachs, lungs, bowels, heart, liver, bones or nervous system. I've had trauma "pulled" out of my lungs, stomach, heart and hips by a shaman. Disease in the body is language. Our story is being told. Our job is to learn to listen. We also need to change our relationship to disease, fever and even aches and pains. They are not "attacking" us. They are not the enemy. We need not declare war on them and treat them as if they are foreign agents intent on destroying us. Instead, ironically, we need to thank them for letting us know what is going on with our feelings, thoughts and beliefs. There are exact correspondences between our trauma signature and how it is showing up in the body. My hips and pelvis are telling a story of emotional and sexual repression.

The Deepest Addiction

Our deepest addiction is to our trauma signature, which we confuse with the "self." We are all "users" if we identify with this self and return to it when we are stressed or triggered, as if it were a hypodermic needle. As we've seen, this trauma signature self comprises our shadow (CUBS) and our false self (CABS), and the leaks are more direct yet unconscious expressions of early trauma.

Our drug of choice is used to support our trauma signature. Initially, we experience alcohol, pot or other drugs as an escape, a way to transcend the traumatized self. With the first few doses (drinks, puffs, whatever), a wave of relief passes over us. We have escaped the prison of the trauma signature! But the next dose, and every one after that, marks a return to our trauma signature. The sadness deepens and we become morose. The anger deepens and the underlying rage surfaces. The self-judgment deepens and we find ways to shame ourselves. We seek to be relieved of the trauma signature but, paradoxically, are also driven to replicate it because, painful though it may be, we are familiar with it. It feels like everything we associate with the name we've been given.

My experience of psychedelic psychotherapy and ceremony work with ayahausca is that the medicine reveals all. The CABs, the CUBs and the underlying trauma become apparent. When we first see them clearly, we feel a kind of giddiness. We're relieved. Everything about our life makes so much sense as we retrace what happened in our marriages or relationships, the pivotal decisions we made at certain stages of our life, the relationship dynamics with family and with our parents. The clarity is such a relief.

This is an important phase. But it's only the first step. As we integrate the depth of the pain that caused us to form our CUBs and our CABs, an astonishment bordering on disbelief may set in. This is what happened for me. I wrote about my night under the stars, blown away by the truth that "my life has not been my own." As the truth of this sank in, residual denial exerted itself. "Could this be true? This can't be true. I must have missed something. I'm making this up. The medicine is playing tricks on me." And so, in my case, it took many, many ceremonies, and many sessions of psychedelic psychotherapy, to accept it.

Once we accept the reality of our trauma, the CUBs and CABs don't just disappear. The work of integration has barely started. We may suffer more than when our trauma signature was in place. For a time after the lid is removed, it can be overwhelming. It was for me.

The Spiritual Ego

Before we turn to how we heal trauma, I want to talk about one way many people deal with the suffering — through a spiritual flight to transcendence. This is a compensation, not true spirituality. When we do this, we are using "spirituality" and spiritual language to avoid suffering. Faced with personal and collective suffering caused by trauma, spirituality emerges as a solution. However, when it does not address our CUBs, CABs and leaks, when it is a substitute for suffering what is ours to suffer, spirituality is little more than an addiction.

The same can be said of psychedelics when they are used only to "get high." Anything and everything, including our own thought processes, can be used to distract us from the underlying truth that was too difficult to bear when we were children.

In his brilliant book *Getting High,* Kester Brewin uses the metaphor of "getting high" to tell his story of escaping his childhood trauma. He comes to understand that his lifelong fascination with flight and space travel, along with his participation in psychedelics and religion, was an attempt to "lift off" and transcend his suffering.

The spiritual ego is just another expression of the false self (i.e., our CABs, but with an overlay of religious belief, whether mainstream or new age). In traditional religious belief systems, we compensate for the absence of our mother's love with another belief — that God loves us unconditionally. Understand, I'm not saying that God/Goddess doesn't love us. But if it is merely a belief to which we give intellectual assent, it will, like other expressions of the false self, fail. The same holds for Eastern-oriented spiritual technologies, such as meditation. We can sit for thirty years on our meditation cushion and experience deep ecstatic states of non-duality. But if we have not done our work with CUBs, CABs and leaks, our state of nirvana will explode when we are triggered in intimate relationships.

This also explains why so many gurus are such pricks. Much so-called crazy wisdom, in which a guru puts disciples through degrading rituals to quash their egos, amounts to little more than self-hatred projected outward. Many male gurus act out sexually, traumatizing female followers. Rarely is it considered that they may be acting out their own early childhood sexual or emotional trauma on others.

True enlightenment requires that we do our underlying psychological work. We cannot do an end run around trauma and expect to be whole. In the chart below I use my own CUBs to illustrate how the spiritual ego can be used as a flight to transcendence.

Core Unconscious Beliefs	Spiritual Ego (Spiritual CABs)
I am bad.	I am a sinner. If I confess my sin, God will love me. I am a righteous human.
I am too much.	False humility. Blessed are the meek.
I am not enough.	I am God/Source Itself.
I am helpless.	Yes I am. But God will be my strength. Anyway, "Blessed are the meek."
It's my fault.	I am a martyr.
Somebody will rescue me (pick up my inner baby/inner toddler).	I am invincible because God will not let me fall. The angels will bear me up.
I'm unlovable.	God unconditionally loves me. Everything is okay.
Life is meaningless.	All I need is the Word of God. The Bible/Koran/Rig Veda is the final authority
My mother will kill me if I don't behave.	The Prince of Darkness waits to ensnare me. If you don't believe what I believe, you are the devil.
I am motherless.	My Father/Mother in heaven never abandoned me.
I'm incapable of love.	Surrender yourself and let God love through you.
I can't support myself.	God provides
I am without hope.	God will make things better.
I am stupid.	All that matters is the Wisdom of God.
Life sucks.	Suffering means that God is punishing you. When you are good enough, God will bless you.
I don't belong.	Your true home is in heaven. In the meantime, you belong to our fellowship. Just believe correctly and act like us and you will be welcome.
I can't have what I want.	I am in a state of spiritual detachment.
I cause your misery.	I need confession every week.

You can see from the chart that the spiritual ego turns God/Source into everything that our parents were not: The heavenly parent provides where our earthly one failed, loves unconditionally where love was conditional in our childhood, rescues us/saves us in our need where our own parents failed, etc. The practices of the faith may confirm our core belief — for example, that I am bad — but they offer a solution: Yes, you are a sinner, but God forgives if you confess your sin. Yes, you cause misery, but if you go to confession regularly, you can live with this belief. It's true that you don't belong, but here is a new family, and by believing what they believe and acting in a certain way, you can find belonging. In this formation of the spiritual ego, the core belief not only goes unchallenged; it is exploited in a way that affirms the need for God and the religion. If the underlying trauma signature were revealed as untrue, the need for this kind of religion and the accompanying belief systems would collapse.

This exploitation of cubs may be why evangelical or fundamentalist churches often thrive where liberal or progressive churches flounder. In progressive churches, traditional belief structures have been deconstructed. The emotional need for God and the church as a rescue service is severely diminished. In liberal churches, people attend for the community, the music, the sermon or the cause of justice. If you walk into a liberal church, you'll never hear that you are a sinner. But you will hear this in an evangelical church, and if you are carrying the cub "I am bad," this is going to resonate. The solution will resonate too: Give your life to Jesus and you will be saved.

Progressive churches can move forward by going one step further. Deconstruct the bad theology and associated beliefs, absolutely. But then deal with the cubs, cabs and leaks. Then true spirituality (which I'll describe in Chapter 17) will come online.

The spiritual ego also works by turning the expression of negative unconscious beliefs into virtues. The inability to self-define and self-express masquerades as the virtue of surrender. The absence of a sovereign self echoes the belief that I am one with All That Is. Deference to others in social situations is elevated to the status of humility. The compulsion to take care of others is celebrated as selfless servanthood. The fear of showing anger is taken to be equanimity. The inability to state clearly what is wanted and to go after this becomes spiritual detachment.

Similarly, the Buddhist solution to the belief that life is suffering (which resonates with cubs like "Life sucks," "I am helpless," "I am unlovable") is to achieve a state of non-attachment. There is a place for non-attachment, of course. Once we get a handle on our unique trauma signature, we can let it go. But again, the only way out of this signature is the way *through*. The spiritual attitude of non-attachment may simply be making a virtue out of the teaching that our desires are bad and unwelcome.

In Chapter 15 I noted how the false self shows up, depending on circumstances, in a depressive form or a grandiose form. As I was writing this chapter, I wondered if Western (Christian) expressions of the spiritual ego represent the depressive form. The CUBS, as I've said, are assumed in traditional expressions of Christianity to be true descriptions of fallen humanity. These are then exploited to make the institution necessary to solve the predicament we're in (salvation). Eastern religions (e.g., Hinduism and Buddhism) do not have such a negative view of humanity. But there is a tendency to bypass emotional and psychological trauma by identifying with Source (Atman Is Brahmin). This identification is seized by the trauma signature, appropriated by the ego, and we have liftoff!

So what is the way forward if you want to get at your CUBS, CABs, leaks and spiritual ego? There's no easy answer, no one-size-fits-all solution. You should avoid any treatment plan promising that you can do an end run around the pain of early failures of love.

My contention is that when childhood trauma is enacted by the very people who were supposed to love you, you will need a loving, supportive relationship to provide a corrective. You can do this work on your own, but in the end it will be tested in the context of intimacy, with either a therapist or a loving partner. And yet, we shouldn't expect our partners to bear the burden of this work. After all, they are often the ones on whom we project our early failures of love. That said, if two people have done this work at some depth, it is possible for intimate relationships to be a place of deep healing and liberation.

In the next chapter I am not giving you a treatment plan or a quick fix. Rather, I describe the stages you can expect to go through on your healing journey.

CHAPTER 17

Healing the Trauma Signature

> *I believe that the most genuine spiritual paths involve a gradual transformation from narrow self-centeredness towards a fuller participation in the Mystery of existence.*
> — **Jorge N. Ferrer, Revisioning Transpersonal Theory**

According to psychologist Jorge N. Ferrer, "The ultimate solution of most religious or spiritual traditions to the problem of suffering is the overcoming of self-centeredness."[27] Stated more strongly, the solution is death to the firstborn self (Christianity); liberation from the self (Buddhism); realization that the true self is Atman (the incarnated manifestation of Brahman); the privileging of ethics, community and relationship over narrow self-interest (Judaism). However this is conceptualized, it is by transcending the self as a self-enclosed entity, interior to the individual, that we achieve liberation, salvation, freedom and happiness.

With the advent of psychology in the late nineteenth and twentieth centuries, and with the burgeoning field of trauma research, we can now

---

27 Jorge N. Ferrer, *Revisioning Transpersonal Theory: A Participatory Vision of Human Spirituality* (Albany: State University of New York Press, 2002).

understand more clearly what exactly is being transcended. I contend that it is the self of the trauma signature that is exposed as a limited and unreliable way of navigating the world.

What follows are eight stages you will go through as you begin the task of healing your trauma signature, as well as a description of the new self, the transcendent ego or Heart Self of participatory consciousness (mentioned in Chapter 5 and described at the end of this chapter), that you are awakening.

Stages of Healing

1. Dis-identify

When we find ourselves in the grips of a memory, we identify with it. The first move is to *witness* what's happening. Using technical language, the subject (the "I" of the memory that we've identified with) becomes the object (the "me" of the witnessing "I.") As we identify with the witnessing "I," we have already differentiated from the memory. There is now space to take control and responsibility. "I have these memories. They do not have me." Once we get that we're in a memory, we do not need to linger in it. Identify it and move on. We need to absolutely decide that this is a memory we are in. Until we are certain, and treat it as such, we will identify with all the feelings, sensations, attitudes, gestures and thoughts that are coming up. We will mistake a trigger (something we are having a reaction to) for reality.

Say your boss at work gives you some feedback that doesn't sit well with you. You remain silent and just "take it." Later, you start to fume. How do you determine whether your reaction is a memory or simply a response that is appropriate to your life condition here and now?

To start with, notice that you didn't ask your boss calmly for more information. You granted your boss an unquestioned authority. In other words, you didn't feel empowered to stay connected until you were absolutely clear about the feedback and what the boss wanted you to do differently. So, right off the top, you are experiencing powerlessness, which doesn't belong to the present reality. Your CUB "I am powerless" has broken through your defense system and is now in full leak mode.

Next, you find that you cannot let it go. It's digging at you. You are digging at it. It preoccupies you. You can't be present for your children or your partner. Maybe you find yourself silently expressing anger at your boss. You tell others how horrible your boss is, trying to recruit them to your side. But you feel helpless to change the situation. You're trapped because you need the money, but you don't want to be there anymore. You find yourself "boxed in."

It's very likely that you have boxed yourself in, reenacting the circumstances of your early childhood, a time when you were unfairly treated, without any chance of escape. At this point, if you can realize that you are in a memory, you can avoid a whole lot of unnecessary suffering. In its place, authentic grief for what happened to you as a child will arise. Then you can take realistic action, as an adult: Maybe ask your boss to clarify the feedback, or look for another job if you truly are being treated unfairly.

2. Mindfulness

We've seen that mindfulness is the capacity to observe our experience in the moment, nonjudgmentally and without attachment. We witness the comings and goings of sensations and feelings, thoughts and beliefs, noticing that we can consciously survive them. Once we did not know this. Now we see that what was once intolerable arises and leaves us, like clouds in the sky. Where we once panicked, we can now breathe.

Take time to notice in detail the feelings and sensations in your body, the thoughts that are arising, the unconscious beliefs that are being expressed, the gestures (body language). Exaggerate the gestures. If your head feels like hanging, let it really hang. Let your shoulders slump, release the muscles in your mouth. If you feel like putting your head in your hands, do it.

If there is a voice of judgment in your thoughts, speak it aloud. For example: "How could you be so dumb?" "Straighten up, you big baby. I'll give you something to cry about!" "Get over yourself." "I'm such an idiot." "What's wrong with me?"

Exaggerate the voice inside that wants to lash out at whoever offended you. "I hate you." "I never want to see you again." "I'm out of here." "What's wrong with you?" "You have been trying to destroy me for years now." "Fuck you."

My wife calls these feelings, thoughts, attitudes and gestures the "bread-crumbs." They lead us back to the experience of the failure of love and the core unconscious beliefs (CUBs) that we formed in response. When we were leaving the treacherous forest of childhood, we dropped them to remind us of the way back to what happened when the time came. The time is now. Try to identify one or more of the CUBs that are in play.

We can re-experience the sensations and feelings associated with failures of love without re-identifying with them. We are doing this work for liberation, not to be re-traumatized.

3. Associate

Inquire into the experience. Remember, this is a memory. It has slipped through the compensatory beliefs (false self) and is directly manifesting as the original trauma. Why now? Can you connect it with a recent experience, dream, interaction, thought, belief? What's happening at work, in your primary relationship or in your friendships? We tend to underestimate just how small a thing can act as a trigger. Why is this particular memory coming up now? What does it remind you of from your childhood?

The step of association is important because if you can connect the experience to something in your present life (and you always can), you don't feel so crazy, as if you are at the mercy of mysterious forces. Association enables you to take responsibility for the reaction. It also frees you from blaming the other person. They or the situation were merely the trigger. They exhibited just enough of the noxious behavior toward you to trigger you and lock you into an earlier memory. Indeed, you may need to challenge the person. On the other hand, you may be able to let it go once you realize that it is a memory.

4. Grieve

Once you see that you are in a memory, having achieved some distance from it and tracked it to a CUB, grief will probably arise. This is the grief that you could not express as a little one, or gave up trying to express because it was futile. You may hear yourself saying things like "Why couldn't she love me? It's not that difficult. Just see me. Feel me. It wasn't my fault." Stay with the feelings underlying these statements. Let yourself feel how lonely, isolated and broken-hearted you were as a little one.

5. Empathize

Compassion for yourself will spontaneously arise if you've felt your own broken heart. Visualize yourself as a child. Imagine that you are the mother or father of this little one. Now is the time to bring all your compassion and love to bear on this little one. Where you-as-a-child were shamed in the trauma experience, reassure your little one that you will never do that. Where you-as-a-child were punished for expressing feelings, let your little one know it's okay to feel everything and anything. Express compassion that nobody was there for you-as-a-child, but make it clear that you are now here and that you will never abandon yourself again. Hold your little one close in your imagination. Be tender, kind and gentle with yourself. Have a bath. Let the tears comes. Feed yourself nourishing food. Get cozy and warm.

6. Connect

Move into connection with another person, a plant, the ocean, a river, Earth or God as you understand Her/Him/It. One of the impacts of trauma is isolation. As you connect, notice that this is a movement in the opposite direction from what Robert Firestone calls "self-mothering" (an unconscious turning away from others when you have learned that you can trust nobody).

Allow yourself to connect in your vulnerability to someone you trust, to nature, or to the God/Goddess of your understanding. I shared my experience of a ceremony in the jungles of Mexico: I felt absolutely destitute and sorrowful. The words "I am a motherless child" surfaced. And then I ventured into the jungle and saw the "Great Mother," the Earth, beneath my feet, the vines and trees. For the first time I understood what people meant by feeling Earth as Great Mother.

Connecting with nature is a good first step. But it is important that you include humans in order to give yourself a corrective experience. Other humans cannot take away the pain of childhood trauma, but they can love you here and now.

7. Ritualize

Make charts of your CUBS, CABS and leaks, similar to the ones that I've shared. This could take weeks, months or years. But once you feel like you have clearly identified your shadow, your false self and how you act out unconsciously, it's important that you commit to dissolving this trauma signature.

This should be done respectfully and with gratitude. The trauma signature represents a core resilience that needs to be recognized and honoured. Like a disciplined soldier, it carried you through the front line of your great battle of survival. But it now needs to be honourably discharged.

This ritual is a commitment to living openly, spontaneously and vulnerably. It is a commitment to trusting your instincts, senses and intuitions. It is a recognition that your Heart Self is indeterminate, fluid and free in how it participates in this life. It is also a recognition that you are the occasion of cosmogenesis — quite literally, the universe was reborn in, through and as you when you arrived.

Now is the time to celebrate yourself as the radiant and unrepeatable soul that you are. You can now proceed in life as though the universe needs you in order to be more itself. You are needed to see, feel, touch, hear and intuit so the world can be more of itself. In turn, your radiant soul comes alive as you are witnessed in your magnificence. You can now love freely and openly and be loved without fear. You can feel your soul as the world and the world as your soul.

You must be witnessed as you carry out this ritual. Invite friends and family. At a minimum, invite one other trusted person to be with you. You might want to make a fire, a symbol of transformation. Ideally, this would happen in nature, near water or in a forest. You may want to call on all the elements, earth, water, fire and air, for support. Include your ancestors. Imagine that they are cheering you on as you end the history of trauma in your lineage and realize something they long for. Call upon any other beings that may be significant for you.

Into the fire, read out your CUBs, CABs and leaks. Give thanks for how they have served you and helped you survive. Place the page(s) in the fire. As the smoke rises, imagine that your new self is rising up to the heavens. Allow the scent of the wood and paper burning to infuse your being. From this point on you are making a commitment that you will live from your Heart Self. Your witnesses are there to support you in this commitment.

This ritual does not mean that your trauma signature is going to disappear forever. But it does mean that you will ask for support when you are triggered and that you will take responsibility for your life in the future.

8. Imagine a New Ending

In Chapter 3 I described how Joan Borysenko teaches participants in her trauma workshops to imagine a new ending to the story, different from the tragedy told by our trauma memory, which is often that we are helpless and powerless. This new ending is different from spiritual bypassing, flight to transcendence, or positive affirmations in that the trauma has been faced and consciously integrated. The exercise rewires neural connections through the use of the imagination. By imagining an old narrative that ends differently — with you mastering a situation, showing agency and success in the face of challenges, and celebrating your power to manifest the life you want — you are honouring your deepest self, which can now come back online.

The Heart Self

Once this work of identifying the trauma signature is underway, a new self comes into play — or perhaps you could say "comes *out* to play." This is a radically relational self, a participatory self that is called into being and calls others into being through deep attention, curiosity and compassion towards the other. The other can be a human, an animal, a plant, a mineral or other element (earth, water, fire, air) or a transpersonal being. As we participate in, and are participated by, the other, a self-in-relation arises in the in-between space, replacing the trauma signature self that is isolated by fear and concerns for survival.

I call this the Heart Self. The Heart Self is never static or predictable. It is emergent, arising in relation to the particularities of the other. This is not the compulsive adaptation of the traumatized self to the needs of the other. It is not motivated by unconscious survival fears. It is the freely offered gift of attention and curiosity, motivated by the desire to know the other. Whereas the traumatized self compulsively uses the other to build itself up or protect itself from the other, the Heart Self is motivated by genuine care. The Heart Self is free and spontaneous. It proceeds in life as if it is needed by creation, and as though it needs to witness and be witnessed by creation in all its forms.

I was recently led through a body-mind-centering process where participants recapitulated in the movements of their bodies the evolution of life from single cell to vertebrate to mammals to humans. By the time we stood up to take in the world as humans, my left-brain way of mediating reality had not kicked in. The verbal-intellectual competency was not operative. I didn't have names for what I was seeing.

In this state, my attention was drawn to a tree outside the window (although I had not yet formed the words to describe it). I had a visceral sense that my attention and curiosity were actually expanding the life force of the tree. It was as if the tree was willing to disclose more of itself when it realized that I was truly enjoying my connection to it. In similar fashion, the tree was participating in expanding my being. We each were participating in the other. I felt as though I was necessary for this tree to be who it is in its fullest expression, and the tree was necessary for me to be who I truly am. I was reminded of the expression "I am through you" or " I am through you, so I," which captures this radically relational and participatory way of seeing and being in the world.

Both the tree and I were caught in the act of becoming, before conceptualization gave what was happening a name. Conceptualization is a critical faculty in itself. Rudolph Steiner writes about how our thinking, naming and conceptualizing completes the phenomenon that has our attention. But this completing activity of mind is arbitrary and reductionist unless we have truly participated in what or who we are giving our attention to.

An indigenous sensibility is that for the sun to rise each day it needs our participation, our praise, our witnessing. This seems superstitious to modernist, left-brain, empirical analysis. After all, the sun comes up all on its own every day without me giving it a thought. But with a participatory consciousness, this is not taken for granted. We need to proceed as though we are needed by creation, and as though we need to be witnessed by creation in all its forms.–

Unfortunately, because the suffering caused by identifying with our trauma signature is significant, we will spend far less time in the dynamic unfolding of the Heart Self that I have just described. We will be trapped inside ourselves. We will rarely see the outside world or other people for who they are because we are so bound up in enacting our cubs. We cannot see the other except as threats or potential sources of affirmation for our ego. In this state, the world serves us, whereas in a participatory understanding of the self, the world does not serve us, because we are not in a deficit condition. Neither do we necessarily serve the world. We participate in the world in a deeply caring way — because we're fascinated by what wants to emerge and be disclosed between us.

Conclusion

What keeps us alive, what allows us to endure?
I think it is the hope of loving and being loved.
I heard a fable once about the sun going on a journey
to find its source, and how the moon wept
without her lover's gaze.

We weep when light does not reach our hearts.
We wither like fields if someone close
does not rain their kindness upon us.

— Meister Eckhardt

We were born for love. When love fails us there is a whole system failure: our bodies contort, our hearts close, our minds defend, and our spirit withers. Perhaps there was an age in the distant past when humans lived closer to Source and knew love was the point of life. But in the modern age we seem to have mostly forgotten this. Trauma is now so deeply embedded in our species that it is difficult to remember what it is to be human, with self and others. This trauma and forgetting are passed down from generation to generation. What we end up with is a degraded normal, a status quo that we defend externally with institutions that perpetuate the violence, and internally with our own carefully designed defense systems. We choose the degraded normal over the possibility of having our hearts broken again.

Our species needs a reboot. My experience is that psychedelics, taken in the context of a sacred ceremony or in a loving relationship with somebody who remembers what it is to be human, can play a role in returning us to our hearts.

This return, after years, decades, and millennia of exile, is a hero's journey, for there is no returning home to the dignified status of human being without grief. The very function of our defense systems, what I've called the trauma signature, is to protect us from this grief. But in the end, as Rilke knew, sorrow is a trusty guide. When we feel safe enough to suffer the grief that was once too overwhelming to bear, compassion arises. We love our self in a way we were not loved, with tenderness, kindness, and respect. We discover our dignity and become an advocate for our deepest longings — longings that were once banished.

The scope of the medicine's intelligence astounded me. Perhaps it is more accurate to say that the medicine opened me to the astounding yet untapped intelligence of Mind, localized as me. It suspended my repression and denial long enough for me to see the truth that I had contorted my life in the interests of survival. It shone a light on all the dark places that I tried to cover up. As well, it reminded me that love, as Meister Eckhart understood, is the point.

The spiritual dimension of this work is particularly clear in ayahuasca ceremonies. This personal work of returning to our hearts, toward love and away from violence, is a work of redemption, starting with our own ancestral lineage. We are the ones we have been waiting for. Before we start meddling with our broken institutions, we would be wise to straighten ourselves up, along with our ancestral heritage. Our institutions will always be manifestations of the state of our hearts. This work is the work of justice, for the cultures and societies we create, along with their institutions, will invariably reflect our hearts.

What of those who hurt us? What is required is a softening. A soft body cannot hold trauma. A soft mind cannot be dogmatic or obsessed. A soft heart cannot help but expand and love. A soft spirit is filled with gratitude and humility. The revenge of a soft heart is a life well-lived, in freedom and compassion. As I've written, this doesn't necessarily mean forgiving our perpetrators. Most of us, after all, are not given the opportunity. But we can let it go. Again, the eruption of grief is the key to this softening and letting go.

On the medicine it becomes clear that those who hurt us were themselves hurt by someone else, and this seems to go all the way back to the beginning. Who knows where it began? Yet to claim that nobody is to blame is too simplistic. It didn't just "happen". Someone did something to cause hurt. We are responsible for the hurt we cause, even if we are not aware of our motivation. Otherwise, there is no basis for ethical accountability. That said, to hold on to blame as a way of identifying as a lifelong victim of the past is unhelpful. The dignity of being human is that once we become aware, we can move on and participate in the emergence of a new future — one that is not determined by past trauma.

This becomes clear on the medicine. Those people who stay on the path for more than a few ceremonies will find themselves undergoing a comprehensive moral inventory of their *own* failures of love — as I did related to the suffering I caused my daughter and the covenants I had broken. I was accountable. Seeing it with such clarity is heartbreaking. It drives us to our knees. In this posture we regain our humanity. The refusal to assume this posture ensures that the violence continues. When our perpetrators refuse to make this journey — one that amounts to ego death — there is nothing to be done … except grieve, let go, move on, and make a promise that it ends with us.

The impulse to ask forgiveness, and to make amends if possible, is natural to the true human, even though unnatural to the defended ego. The refusal to do so is at the root of the perpetuation of violence. At some point, in one lifetime or another, perpetrators of family violence will discover how they have failed themselves, in the first place as souls made in the image of their Creator, and then as stewards of children. This sullying of our sacred nature is why the practice of purification is inherent to all religions and ancient indigenous traditions.

Healing is possible. It takes a dismantling of the life we thought was ours, a dying to "me" and a resurrection of "I", again and again. With the time we have left we may make a true offering of our unrepeatable life to this beautiful world. We can exit the hypnotic trance that our families may have unwittingly induced, supported by societal institutions dedicated to our entrancement. It is possible to gain the freedom that is the fruit of taking radical responsibility for our lives. Nobody outside of you or me can determine our degree of happiness or the freedom to proceed as if we matter. We can recover the inherent intensity of life, which appears as the absolute value and mystery of life, this life, the one we have been given to live. We can rediscover gratitude for being given the opportunity. We can become lovers again, of the whole of it, of every grain of sand and every leaf, and even, by grace and much grief, of those who failed us.

Bibliography

Bortoft, Henri. *Taking Appearances Seriously: The Dynamic Way of Seeing in Goethe and European Thought.* Edinburgh: Floris Books, 2012.

Brewin, Kester. *Getting High: A Savage Journey to the Heart of the Dream of Flight.* London: Vaux Publishing, 2016.

Buber, Martin. *I and Thou.* New York: Charles Scribner's Sons, 1958.

De Alverga, Alex Polari. *The Religion of Ayahuasca: The Teachings of the Church of Santo Daime.* Rochester, NY: Vermont Park Street Press, 2010.

Elenbass, Adam. *Fishers of Men: The Gospel of an Ayahuasca Vision Quest.* New York: Jeremy P. Tarcher/Penguin, 2010.

Ferrer, Jorge N. *Revisioning Transpersonal Theory: A Participatory Vision of Human Spirituality.* Albany: State University of New York Press, 2002.

Firestone, W. Robert. *The Fantasy Bond: The Structure of Psychological Defenses.* New York: Human Sciences Press, 1985.

Forward, Susan. *Mothers Who Can't Love: A Healing Guide for Mothers and Daughters.* New York, New York: Harper Press, 2013.

Friedman, Gil. *Gurdjieff: A Beginner's Guide.* Friedman, 2011.

Gray, Stephen. *Returning to the Sacred World: A Spiritual Toolkit for the Emerging Reality.* The Bothy, UK: O-Books, 2010.

Grof, Stan. *Healing Our Deepest Wounds: The Holotropic Paradigm Shift.* Rochester, VT: Newcastle, Washington Stream of Experience Productions, 2012.

Grof, Stan. *LSD Doorway to the Numinous: The Groundbreaking Psychedelic Research into Realms of the Human Unconscious.* South Paris, ME: Park Street Press, 1975.

Herman, Judith. *Trauma and Recovery: The Aftermath of Violence from Domestic Abuse to Political Terror.* New York: Basic Books, 1992.

Heschel, Abraham. *God in Search of Man: A Philosophy of Judaism.* New York: Farrar, Straus, Giroux, 1955.

Huxley, Aldous. *The Doors of Perception.* New York: Harper and Brothers, 1954.

Kalef, Mia. *The Secret Life of Babies: How Our Prebirth and Birth Experiences Shape Our World.* Berkeley, CA: North Atlantic Books, 2014.

Lachman, Gary. *Caretakers of the Cosmos: Living Responsibly in an Unfinished World.* Edinburgh: Floris Books, 2013.

Lachman, Gary. *A Secret History of Consciousness.* Great Barrington, MA: Lindisfarne Press, 2003.

Lachman, Gary. *Secret Teachers of the Western World.* New York: Jeremy Tarcher/Penguin, 2015.

Laing, R. D. *The Politics of Experience and the Bird of Experience.* New York: Penguin Group, 1967

Laing, R. D. *The Politics of Family and Other Essays.* New York: Vintage Books, 1972.

Large, William. *Levinas' Totality and Infinity.* London: Bloomsbury Academic, 1969.

Lamott, Anne. *Bird by Bird: Some Instructions On Writing and Life.* New York: Anchor Books, 1995.

Levinas, Emmanuel. *Totality and Infinity: An Essay On Exteriority.* Pittsburgh, PA: Duquesne University Press, 1961.

Levine, Peter. *Waking the Tiger: Healing Trauma.* Berkeley, CA: North Atlantic Books, 1997.

Miller, Alice. *The Drama of the Gifted Child: The Search for the True Self.* New York: Basic Books, 1981.

Miller, Alice. *For Your Own Good: Hidden Cruelty in Childhood and the Roots of Violence.* New York: Farrar, Straus, Giroux, 1984.

Miller, Alice. *The Truth Shall Set You Free: Overcoming Emotional Blindness and Finding Your True Adult Self.* New York: Basic Books, 2001.

Morgan, L. Michael. *The Cambridge Introduction to Emmanuel Levinas.* Cambridge: Cambridge University Press, 2011.

Ouspensky, P. D. *In Search of the Miraculous: Fragments of an Unknown Teaching.* London: Routledge and Kegan Paul, 1950.

Rush, Florence. *The Best-Kept Secret: Sexual Abuse of Children.* New York: McGraw-Hill, 1980.

Sessa, Ben. *Psychedelic Drug Treatments: Assisting the Therapeutic Process.* Dulles, VA: Muswell Hill Press, 2013.

Shanon, Benny. *The Antipodes of the Mind: Charting the Phenomenology of the Ayahuasca Experience.* New York: Oxford University Press, 2002.

Shroder, Tom. *Acid Test: LSD, Ecstasy and the Power to Heal.* New York: Plume Books, 2015.

Steiner, Rudolph. *The Philosophy of Freedom: The Basis for a Modern World Conception.* Germany: Rudolph Steiner Press, 1896.

Strassman, Rick. *DMT: The Spirit Molecule.* Rochester, VT: Park Street Press, 2000.

van der Kolk, Bessel. *The Body Keeps Score: Brain, Mind and Body in the Healing of Trauma.* New York: Penguin Books, 2014.

van Kampenhout, Daan. *The Tears of the Ancestors: Victims and Perpetrators in the Tribal Soul.* Phoenix, AZ: Zeig, Tucker and Theisen, 2008.

Wilson, Colin. *The New Existentialism.* New York: HarperCollins, 1966.

Wilson, Colin. *Superconsciousness: The Quest for Peak Experience.* London: Watkins Publishing, 2009.

Wink, Walter. *Unmasking the Powers: The Invisible Forces That Determine Human Existence.* Minneapolis, MN: Fortress Press, 1986.

Wolynn, Mark. *It Didn't Start with You: How Inherited Family Trauma Shapes Who We Are and How to End the Cycle.* New York: Viking, 2016.

About the Author

Bruce Sanguin is a psychotherapist living on an island in the Pacific Northwest with his wife, Mia, and his dog Koa. Formerly he was a minister in the United Church of Canada. He has written six other books in the area of evolutionary spirituality. His clients travel to the island to make intensive journeys with him as well as do sessions by Skype. Bruce regularly blogs at www.brucesanguin.ca.

All inquiries related to speaking invitations, intensives, or setting up a session with Bruce should be directed to bsanguin@telus.net.

If you enjoyed the book please write a review on Amazon.com.

Other Works by Bruce Sanguin

The Way of the Wind: The Path and Practice of Evolutionary Mysticism, 2015. (Winner of the Jenkins Medal Award in the category of Spiritual Book)

The Emerging Church: A Model for Change and a Map for Renewal, Expanded And Revised, 2014.

Painting the Stars: Religion and Evolving Faith (participant's manual and featured presenter)

The Advance of Love: Reading the Bible with An Evolutionary Heart, 2012.

If Darwin Prayed: Prayers for Evolutionary Mystics, 2011. (IPPY Gold Medal Award for best spiritual book of 2011).

Experiencing Ecological Christianity, 2011. Tim Scorer and Bruce Sanguin. (Study guide for *Darwin, Divinity, and the Dance of the Cosmos*).

Darwin, Divinity and the Dance of the Cosmos; An Ecological Christianity, 2007.

Summoning the Whirlwind, Unconventional Sermons for a Contemporary Christian Faith, 2005.